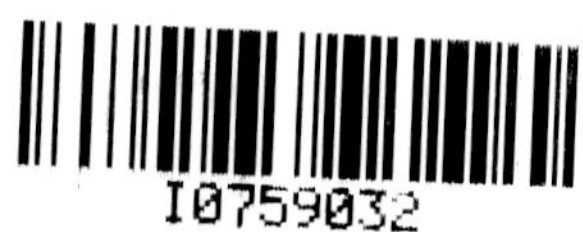

This books belongs to

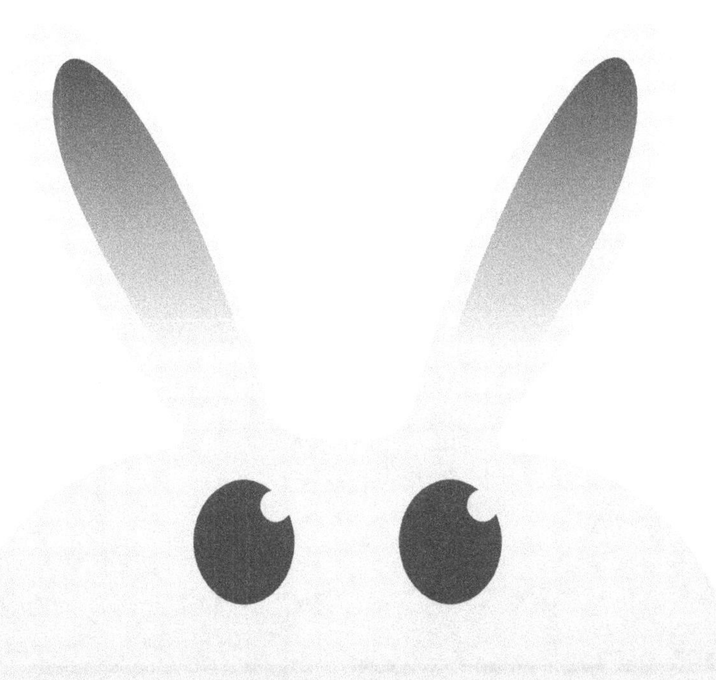

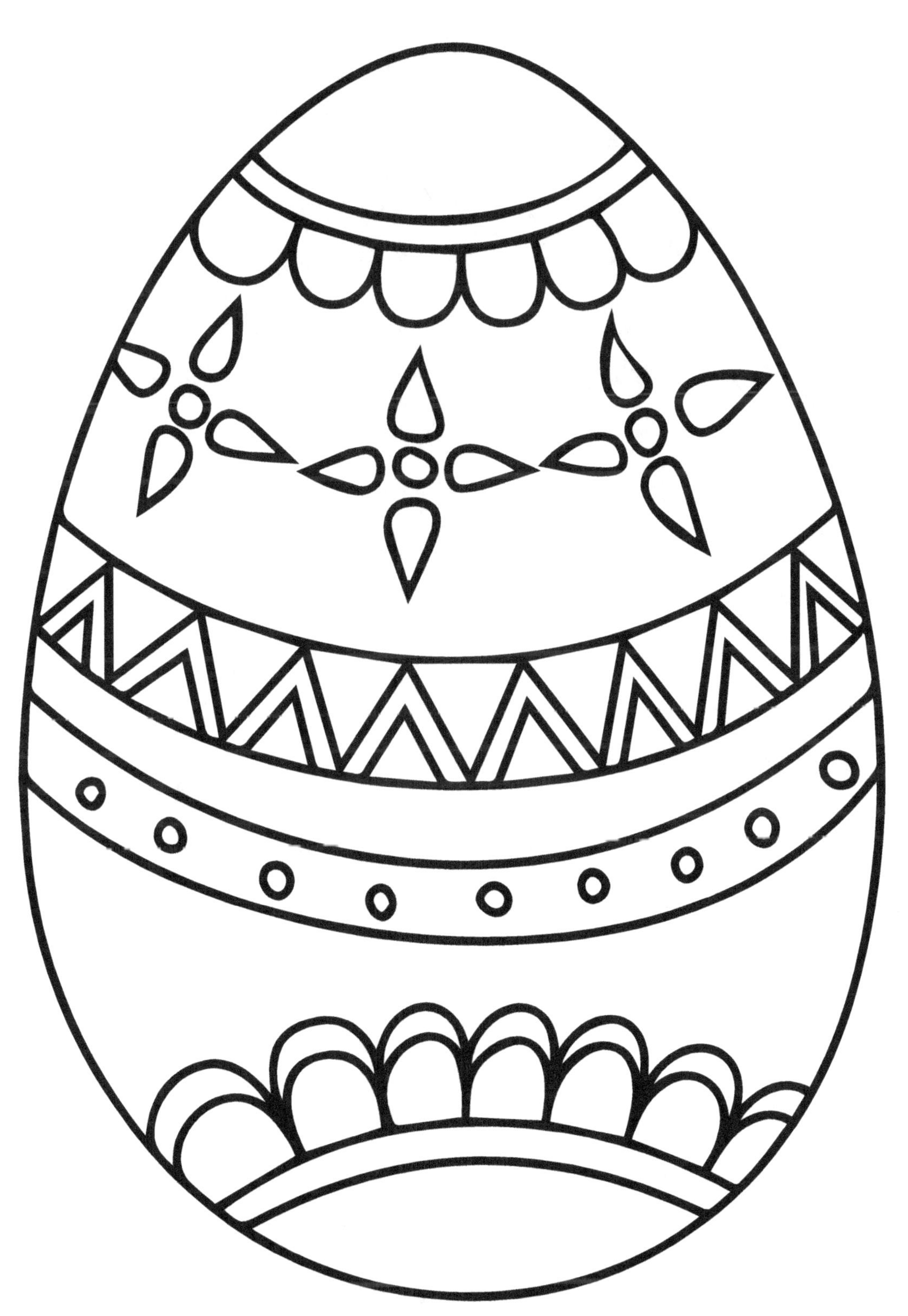

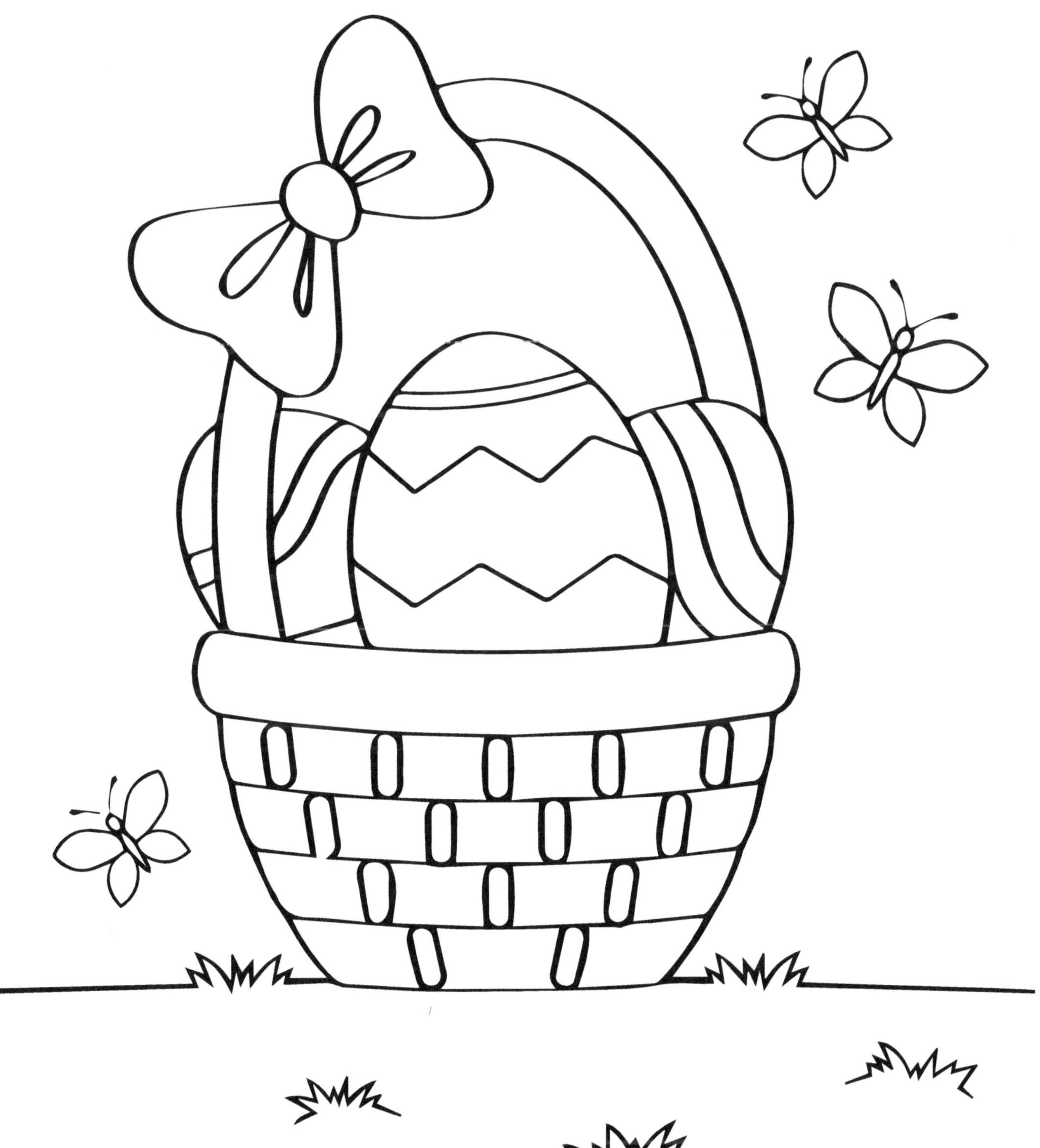

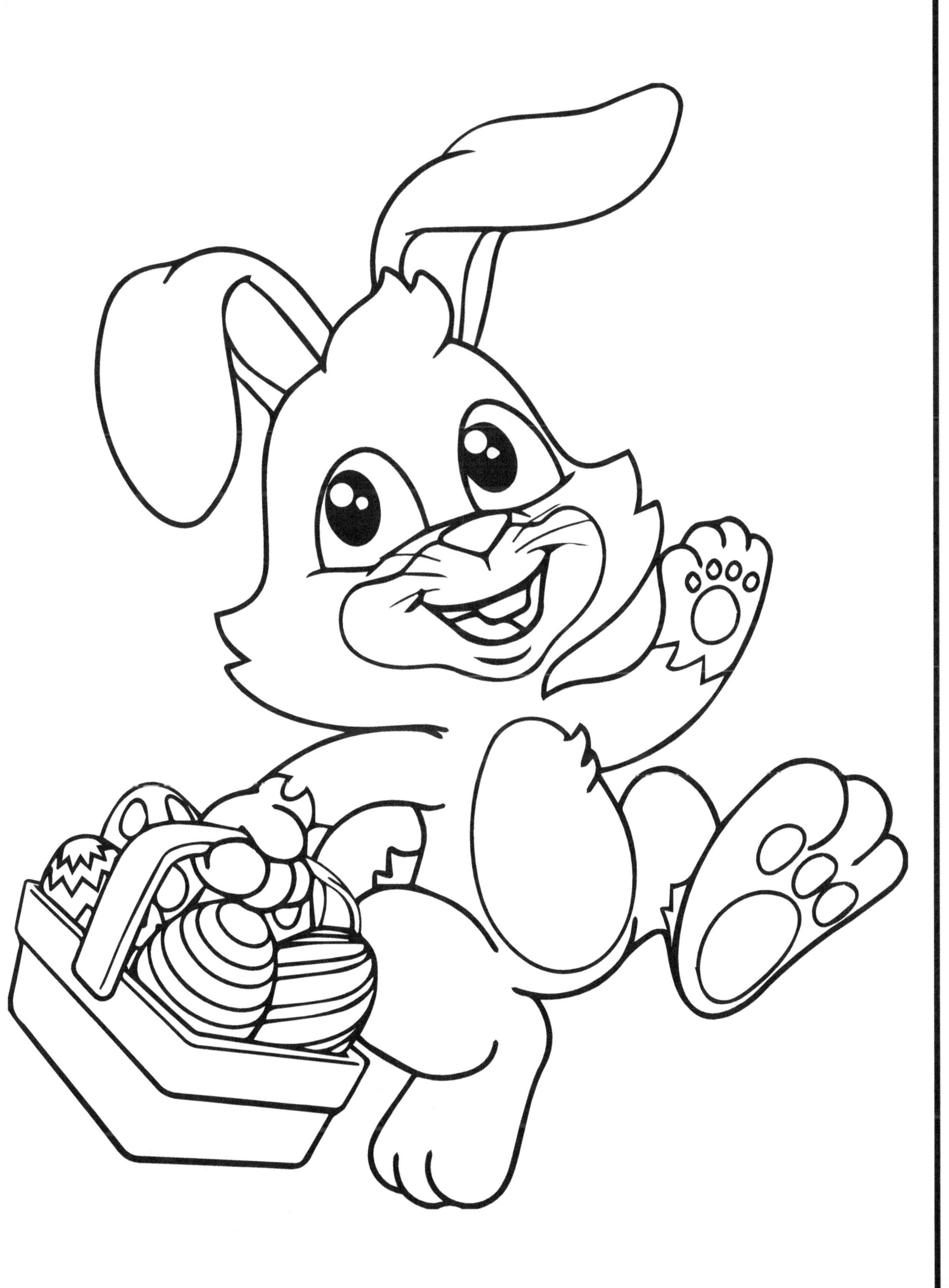

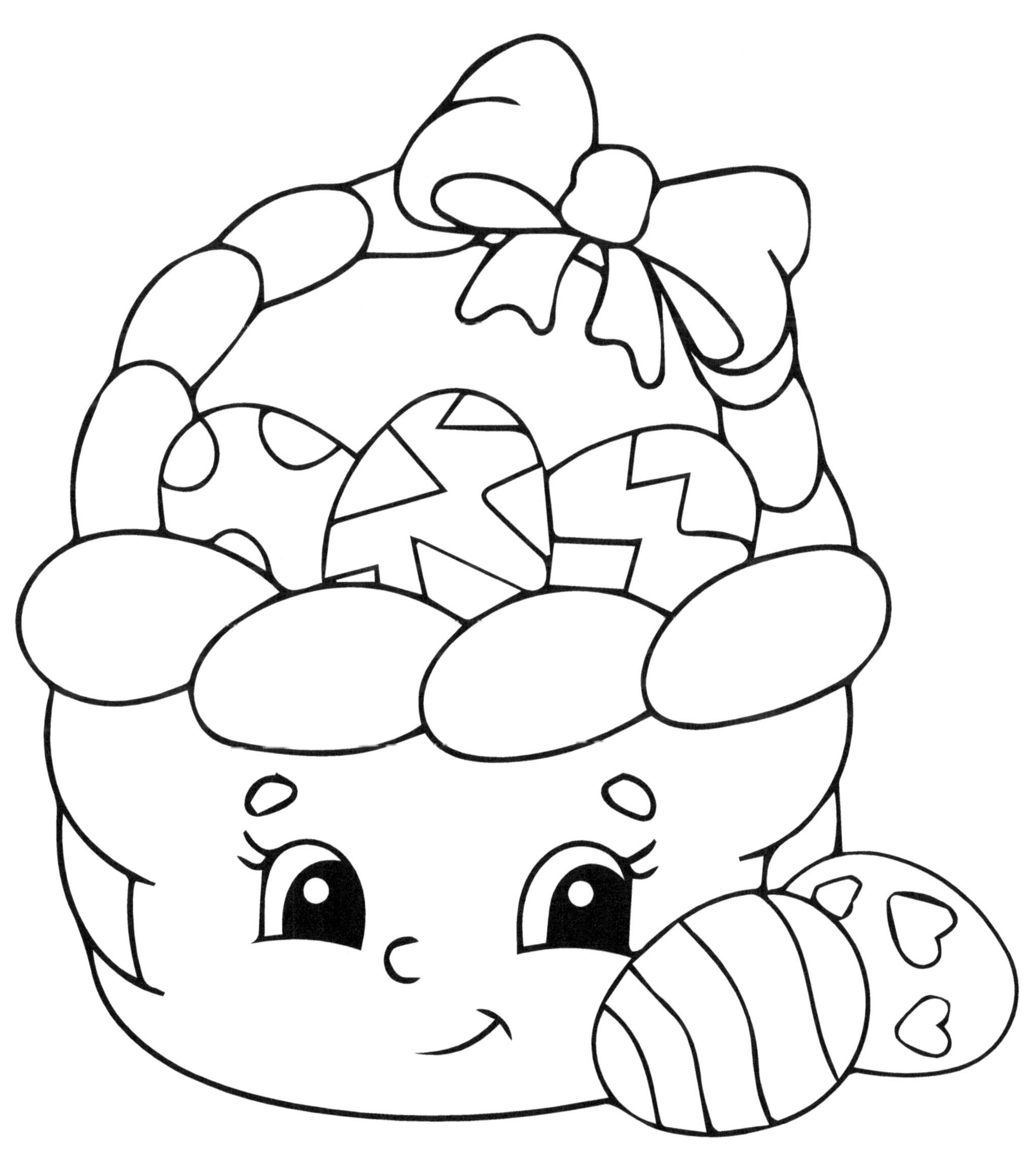

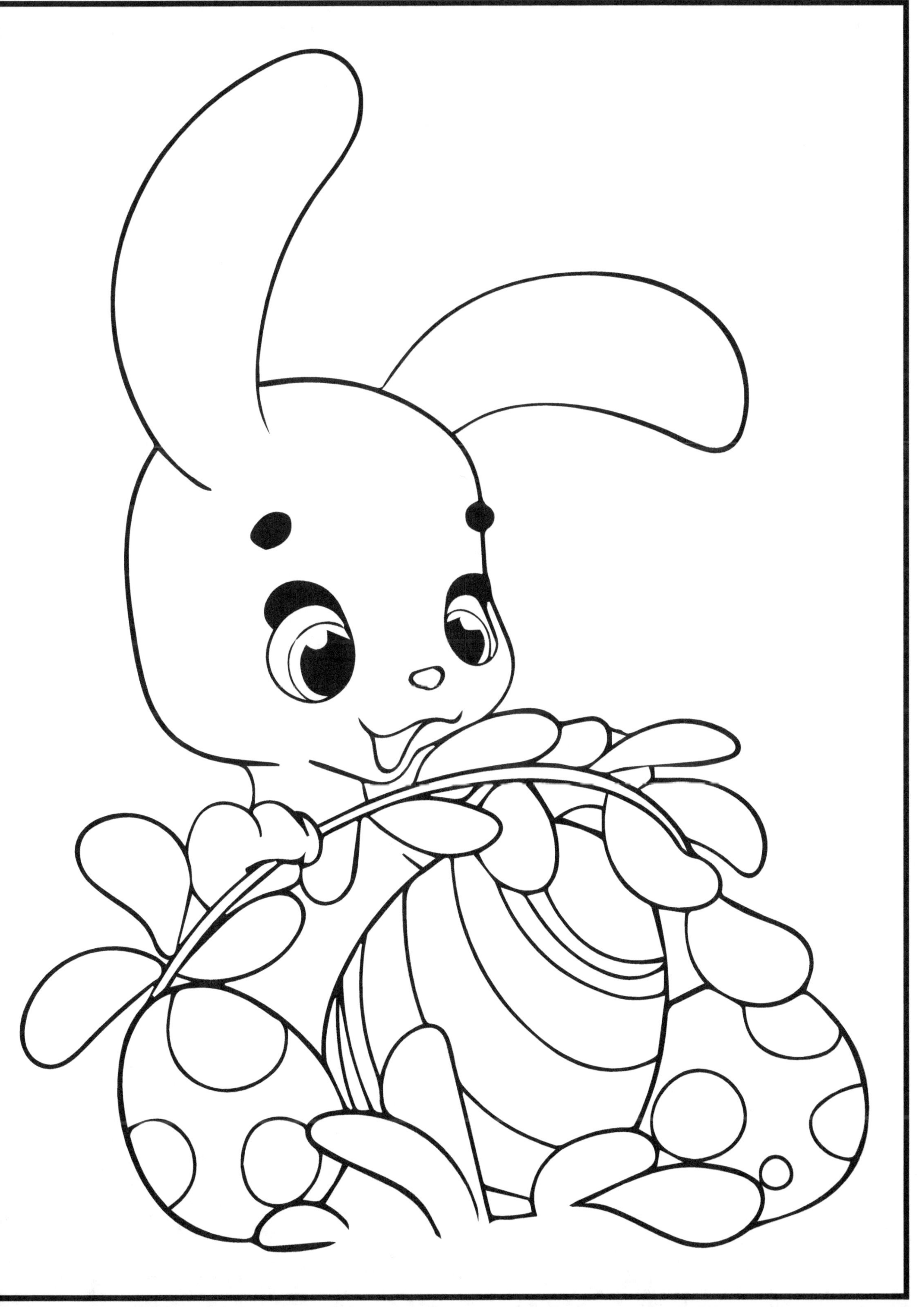

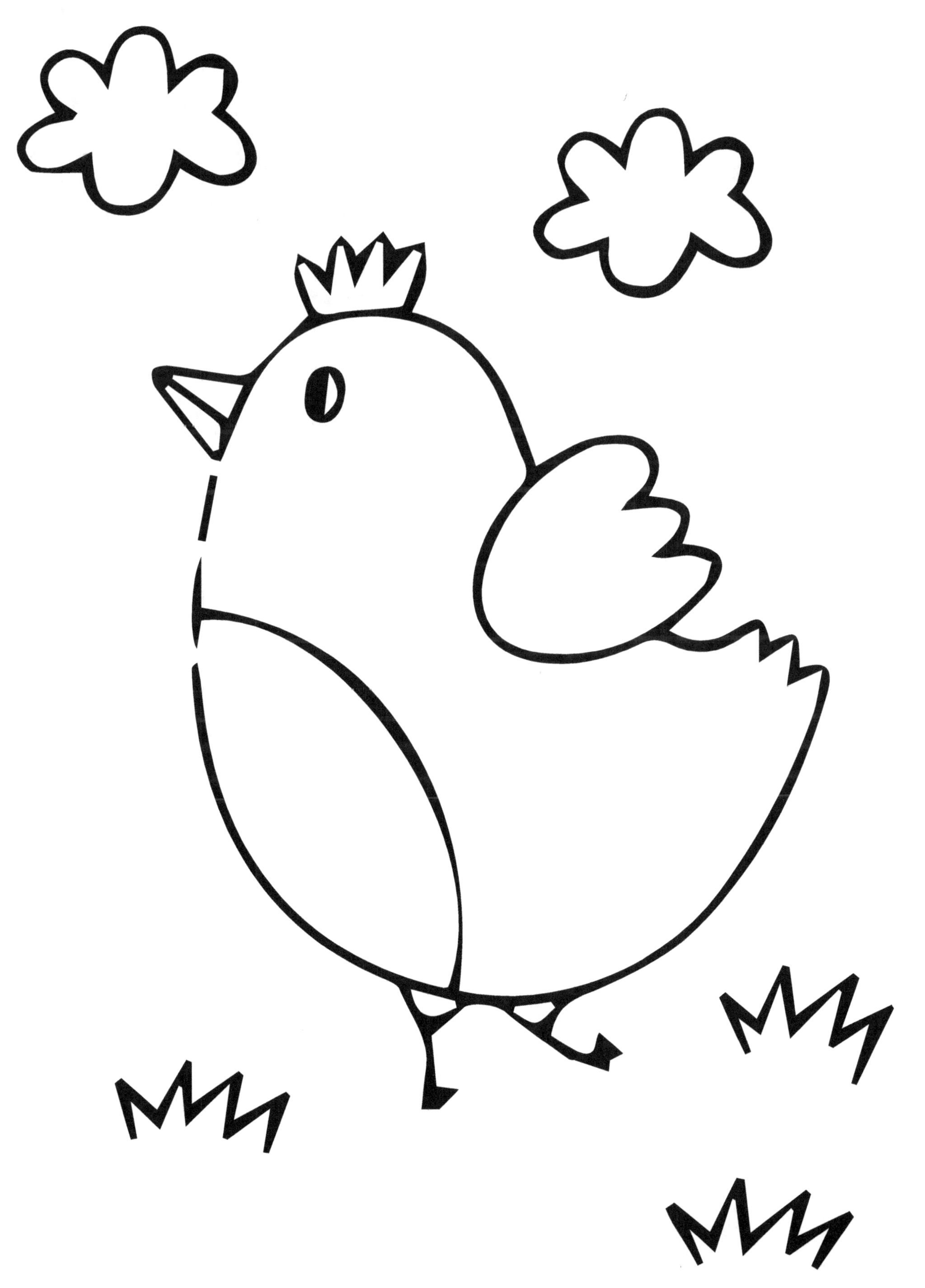

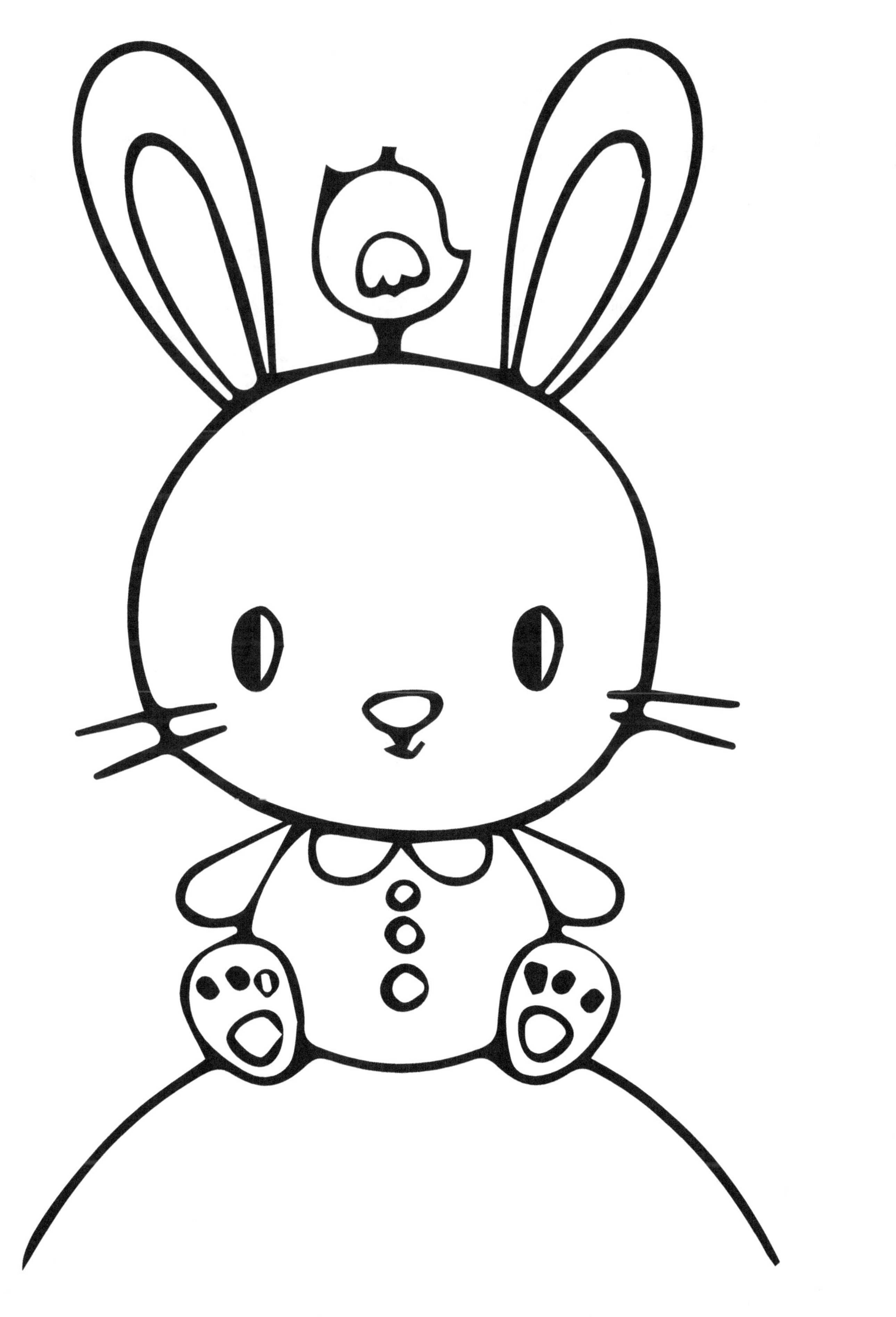

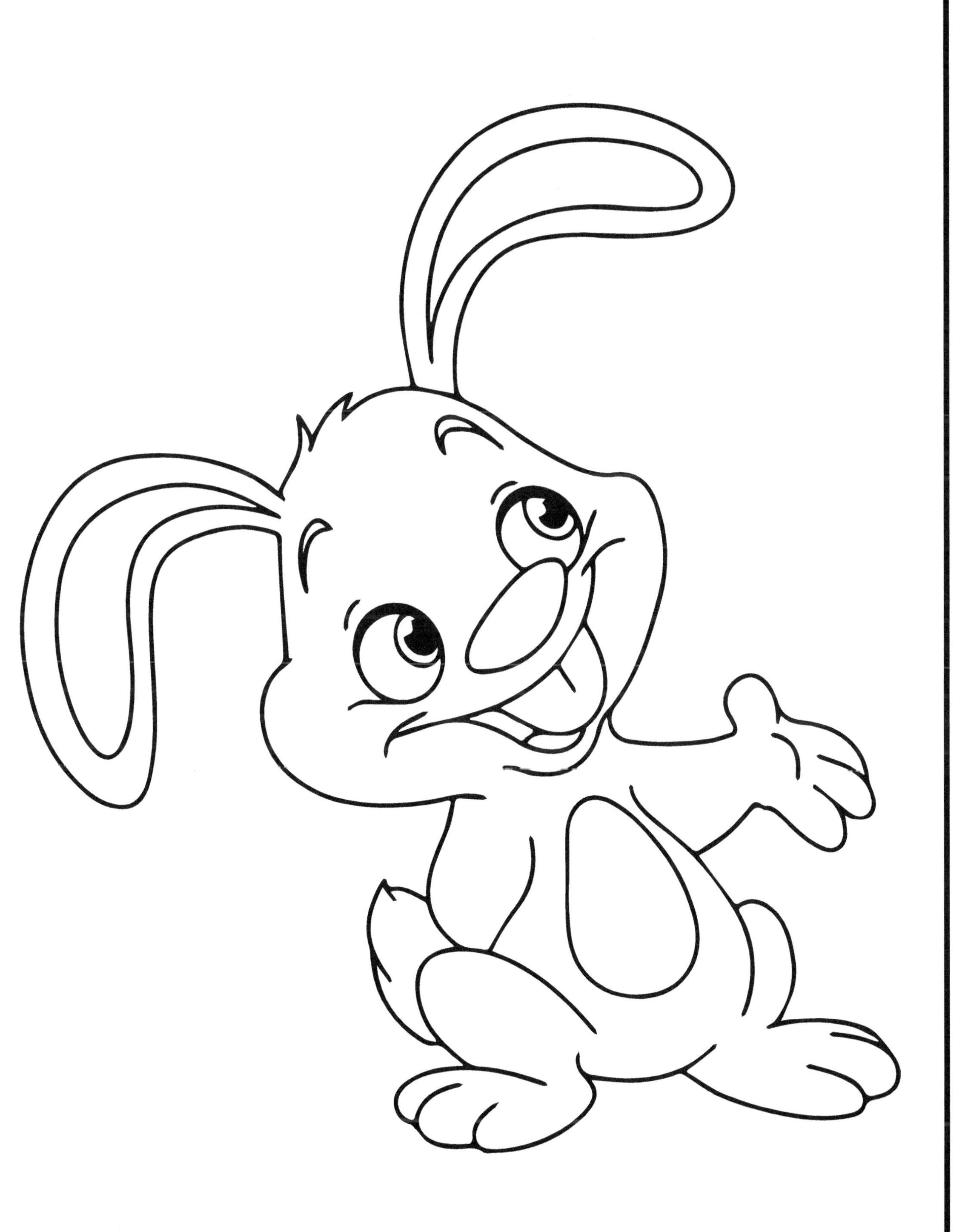

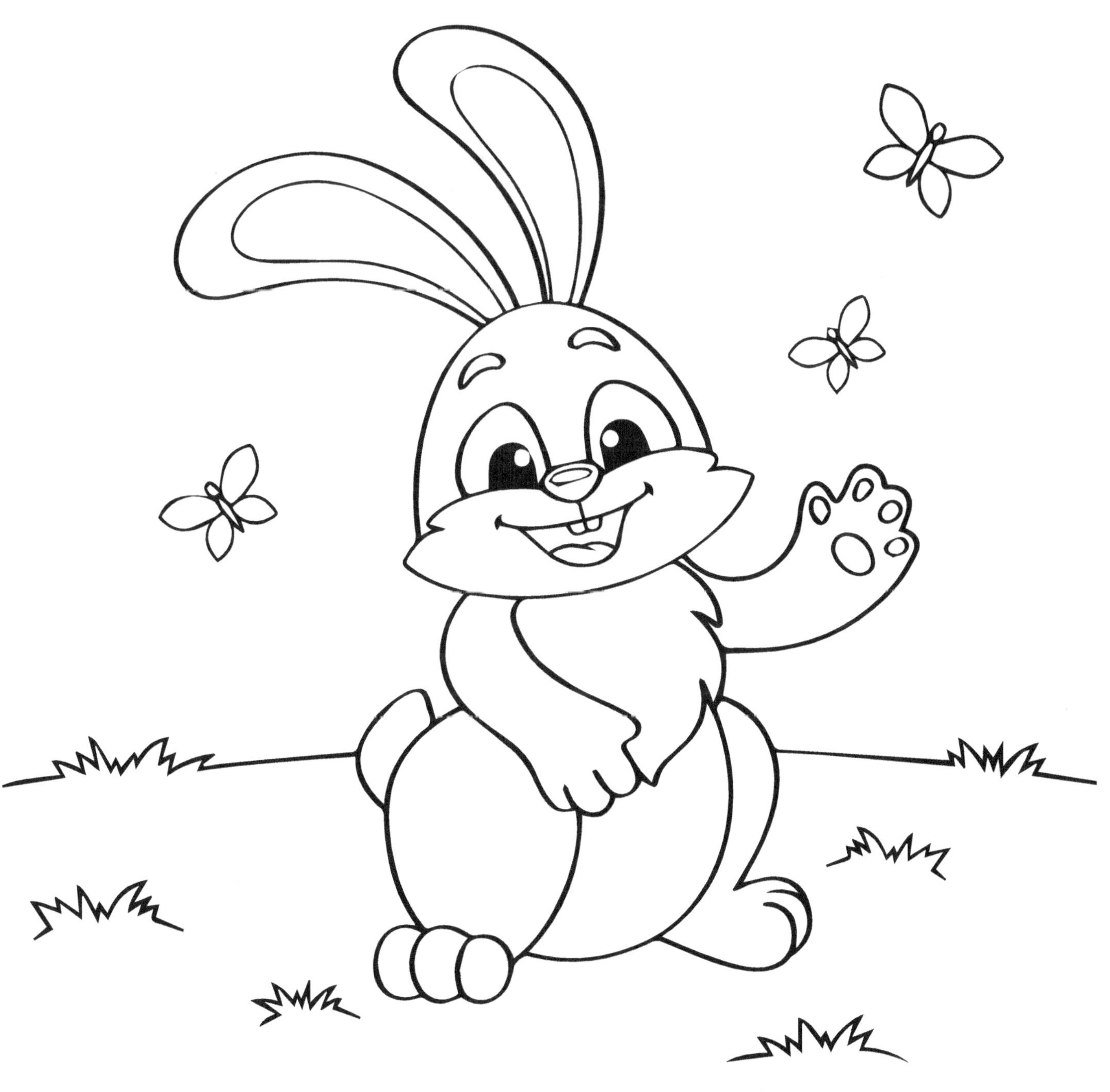

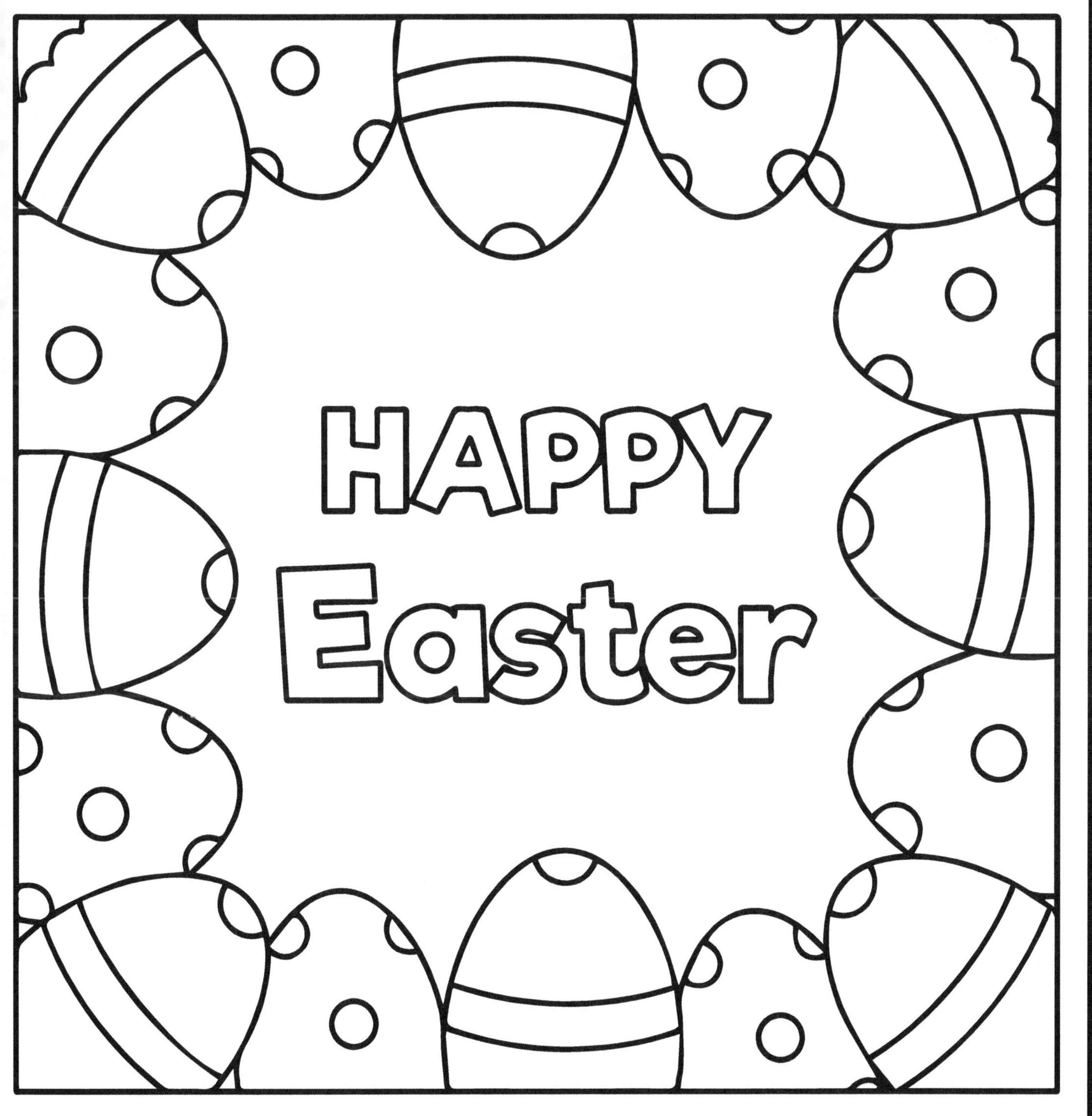

HAPPY
Easter

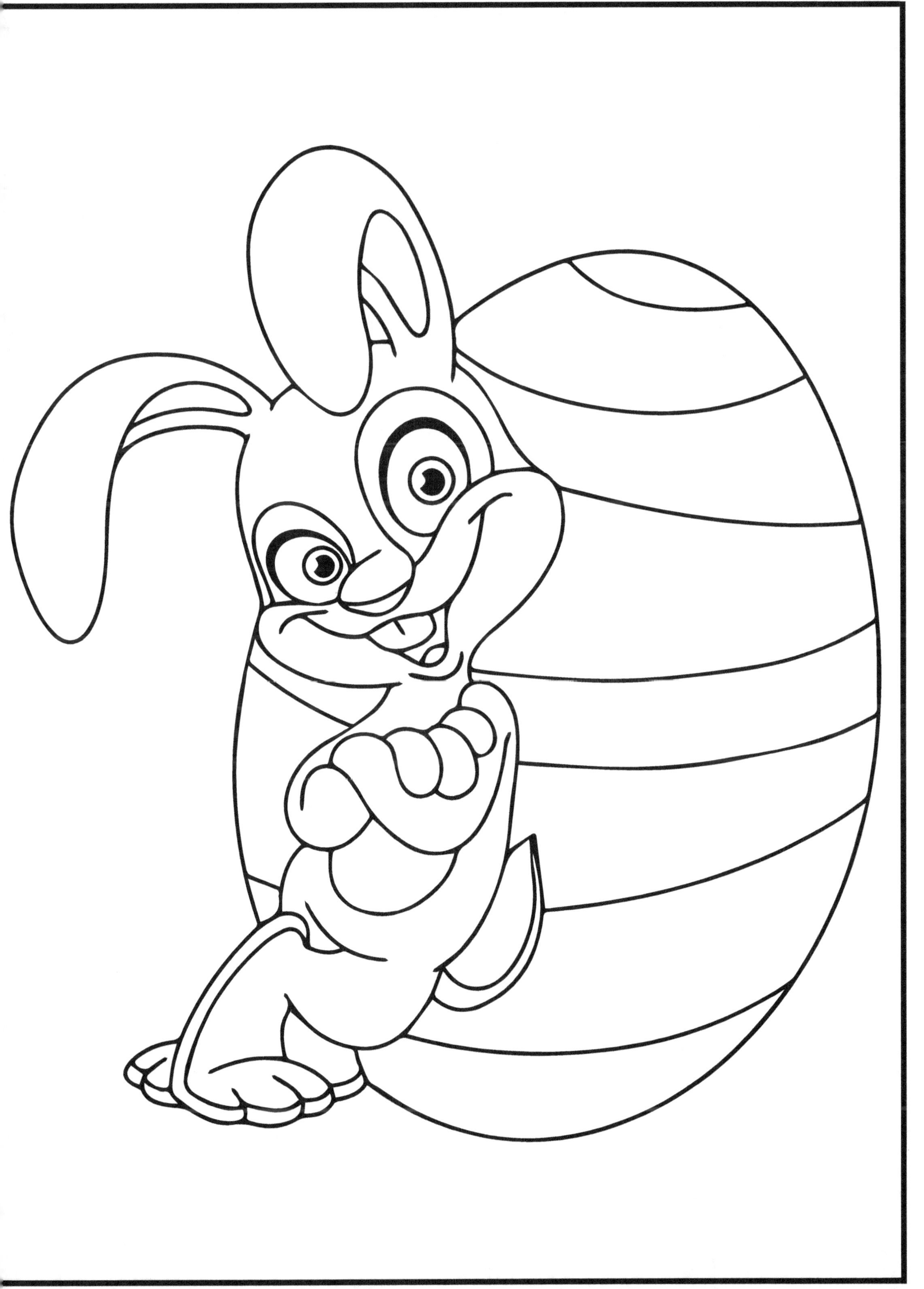

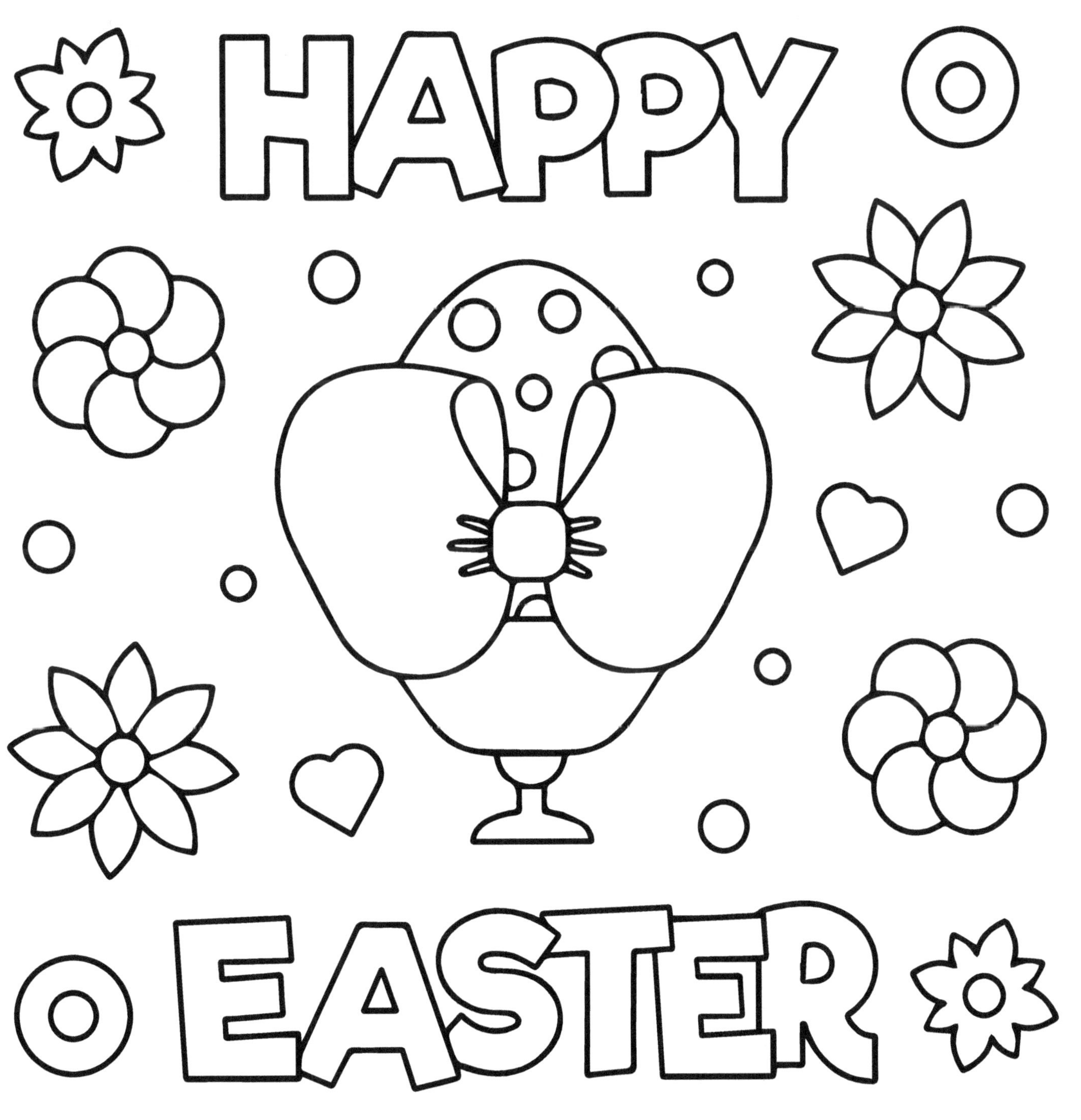

HAPPY
EASTER

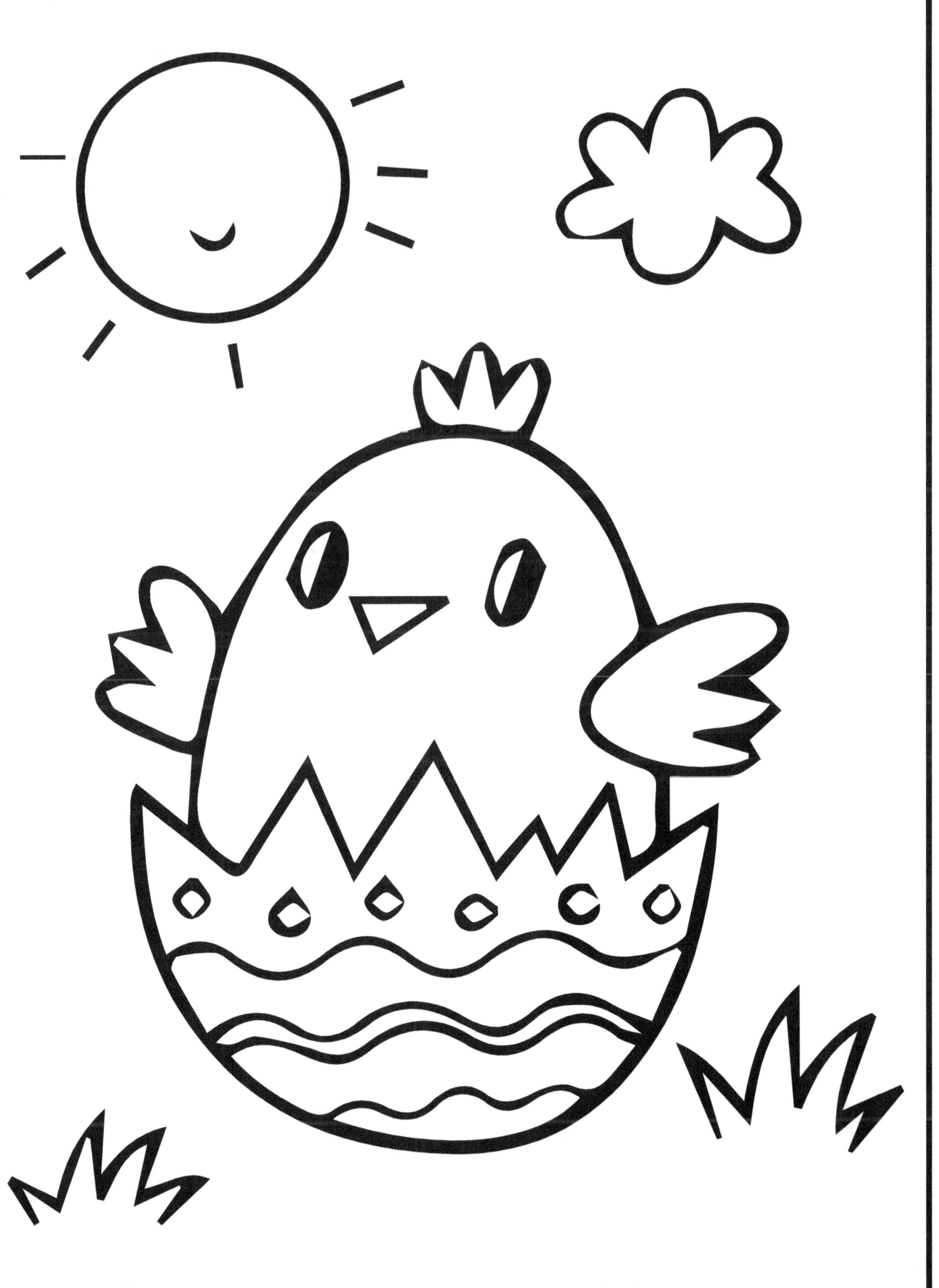

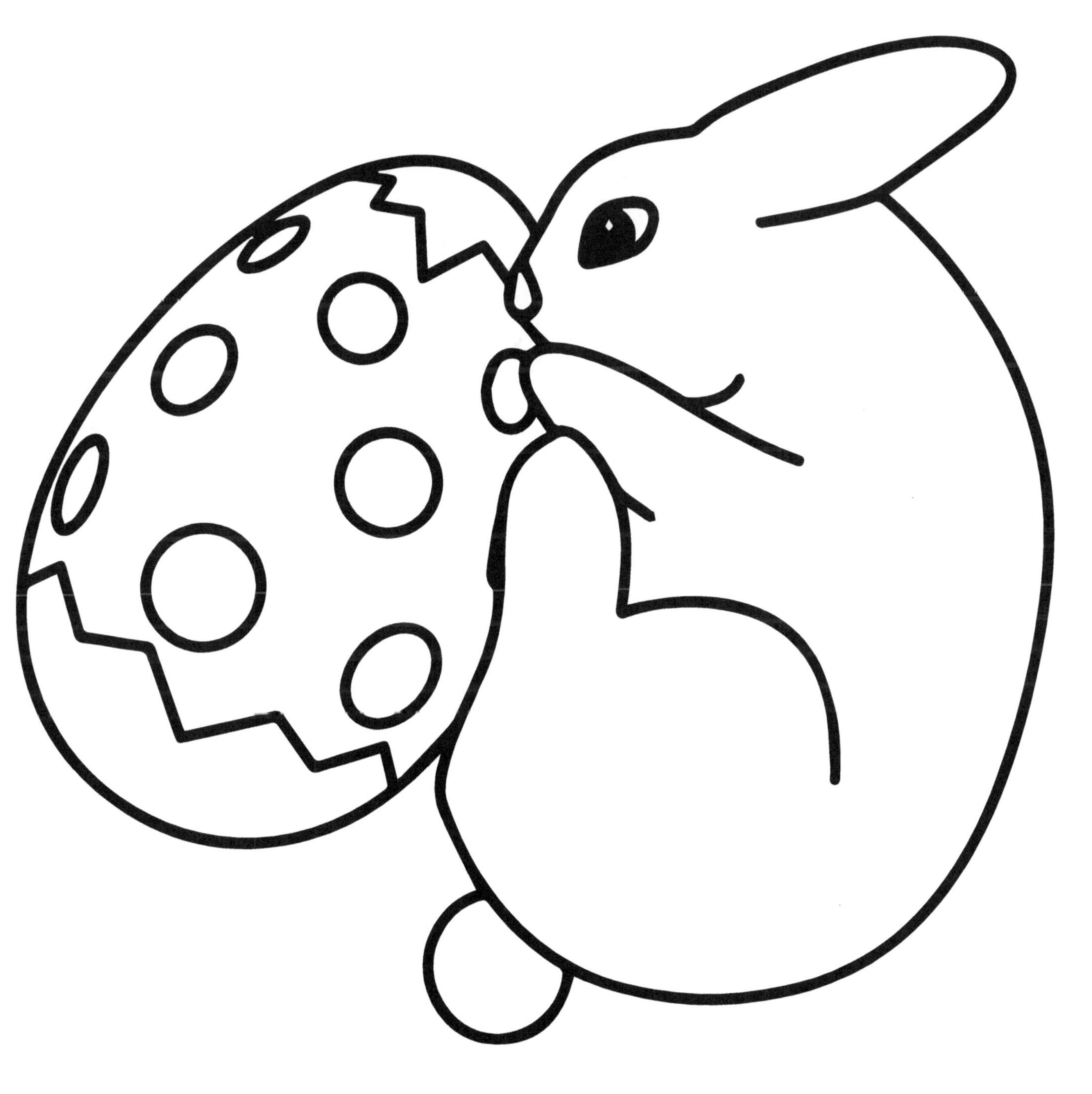

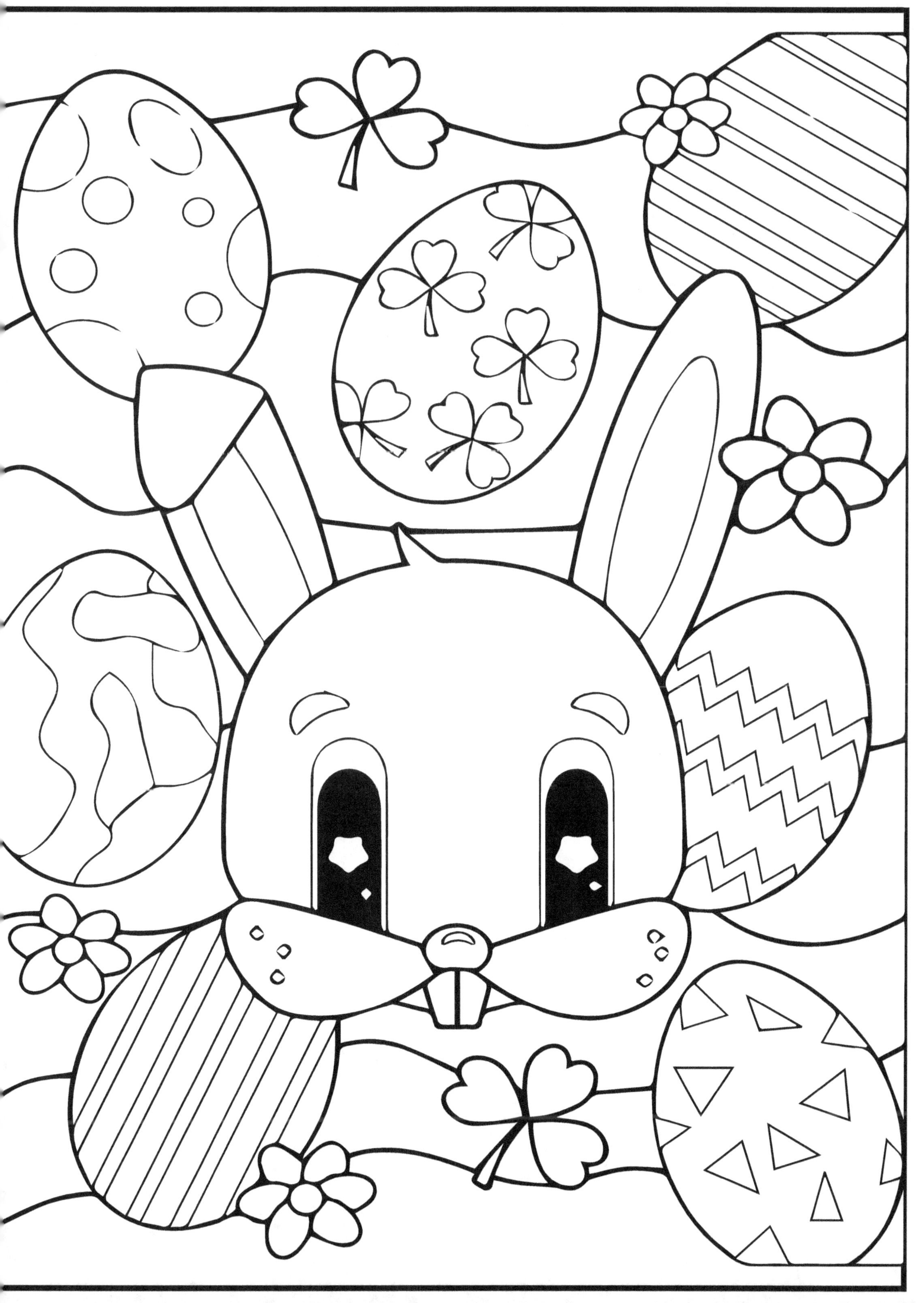

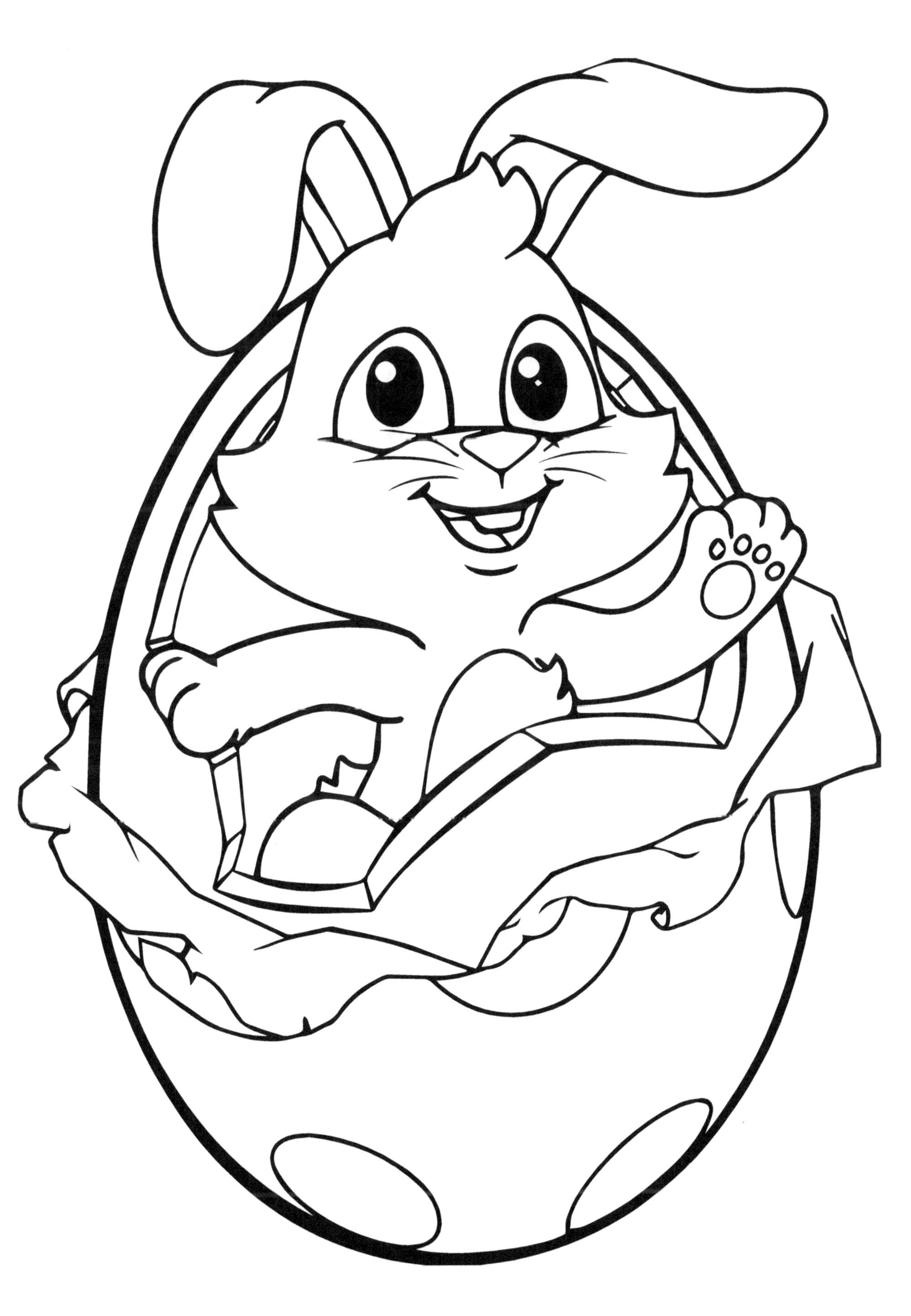

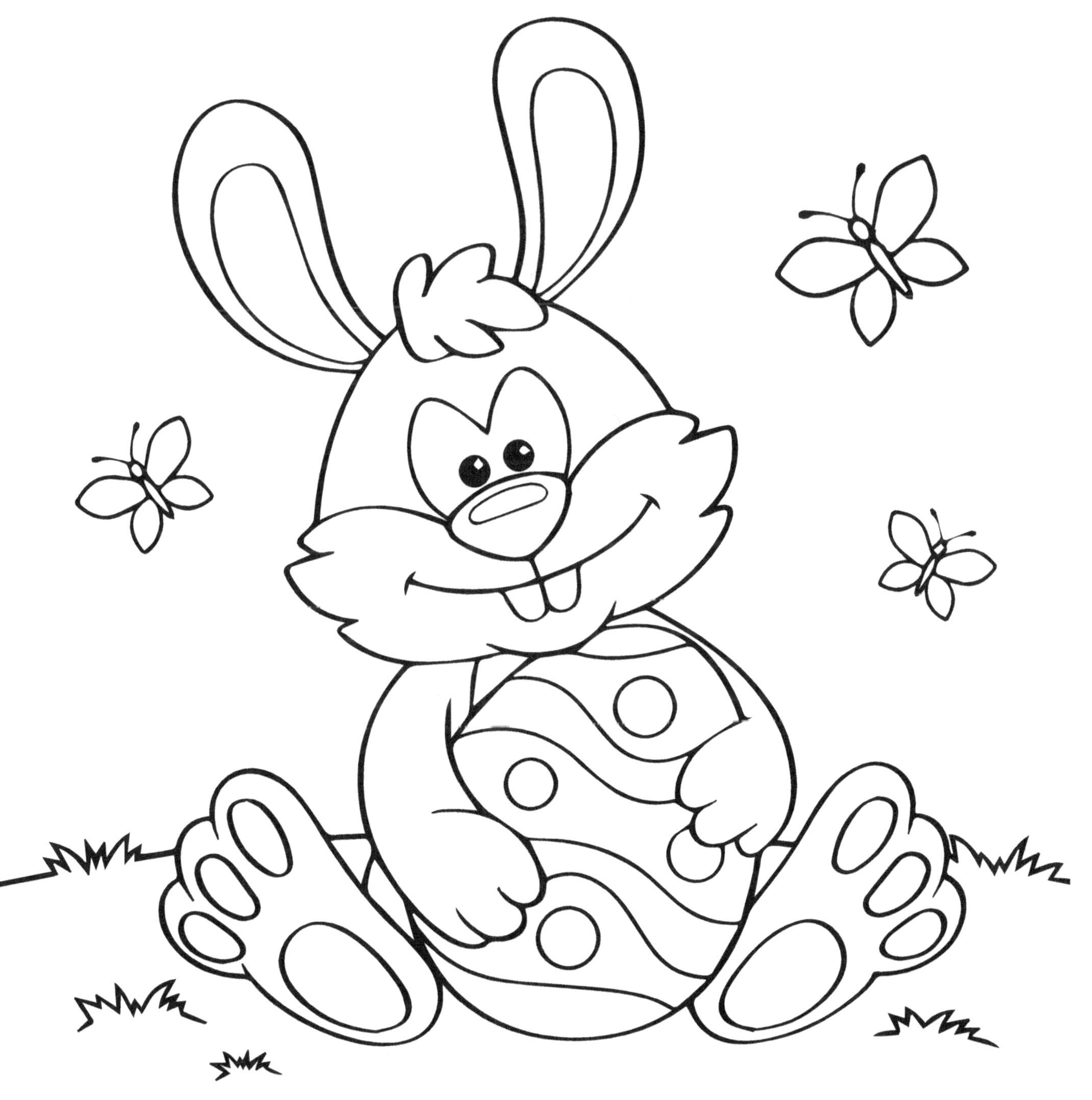

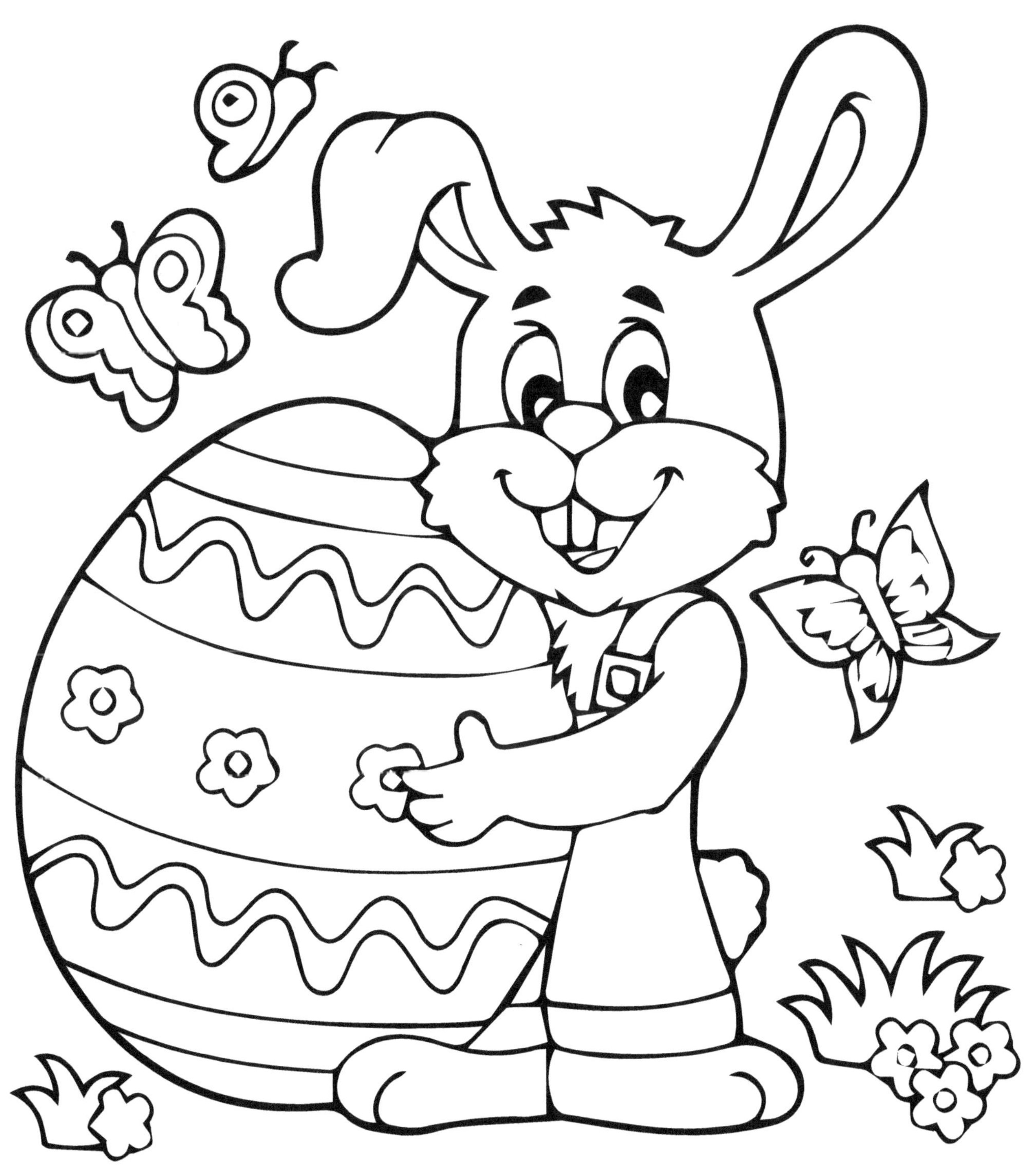

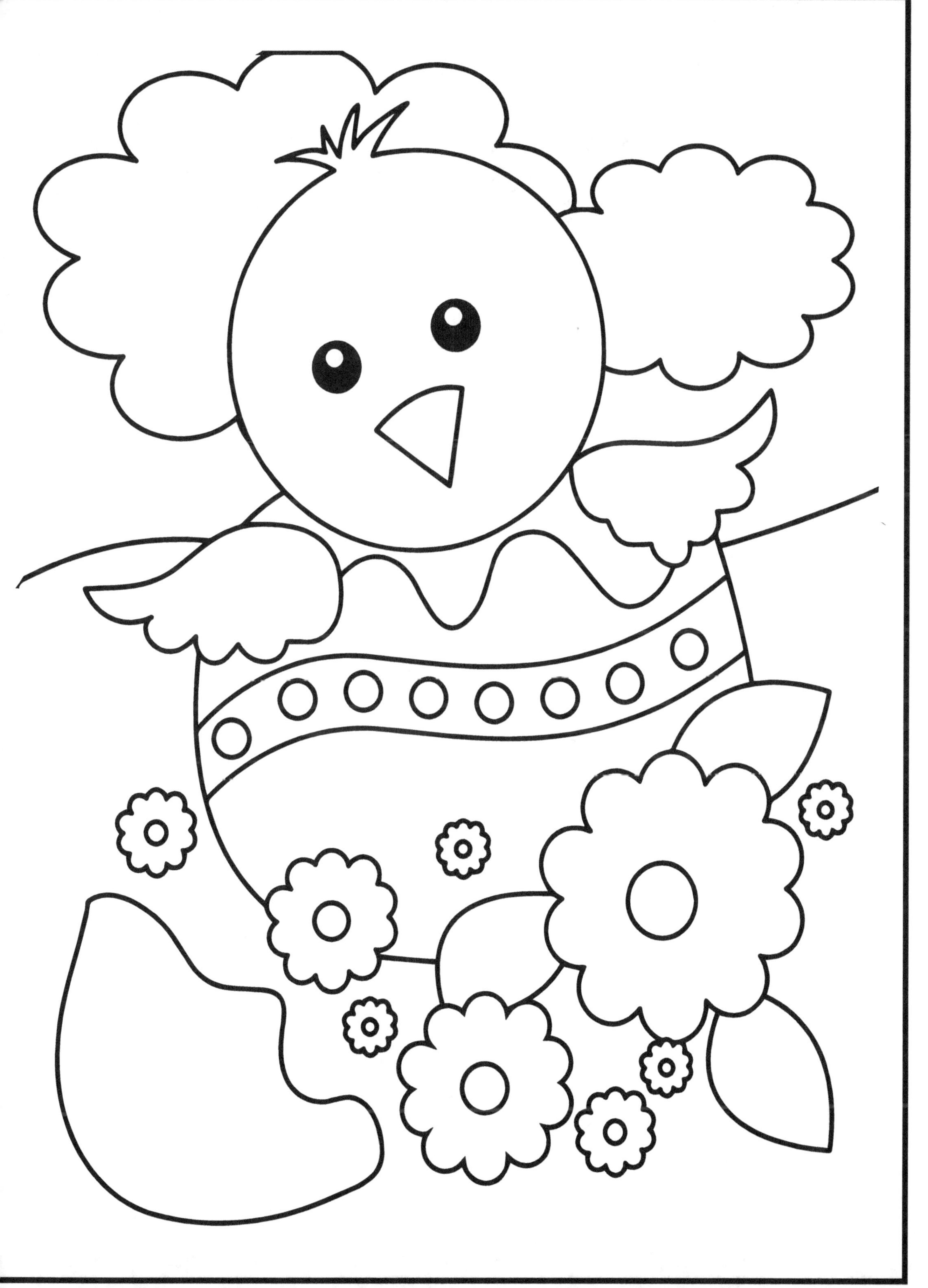

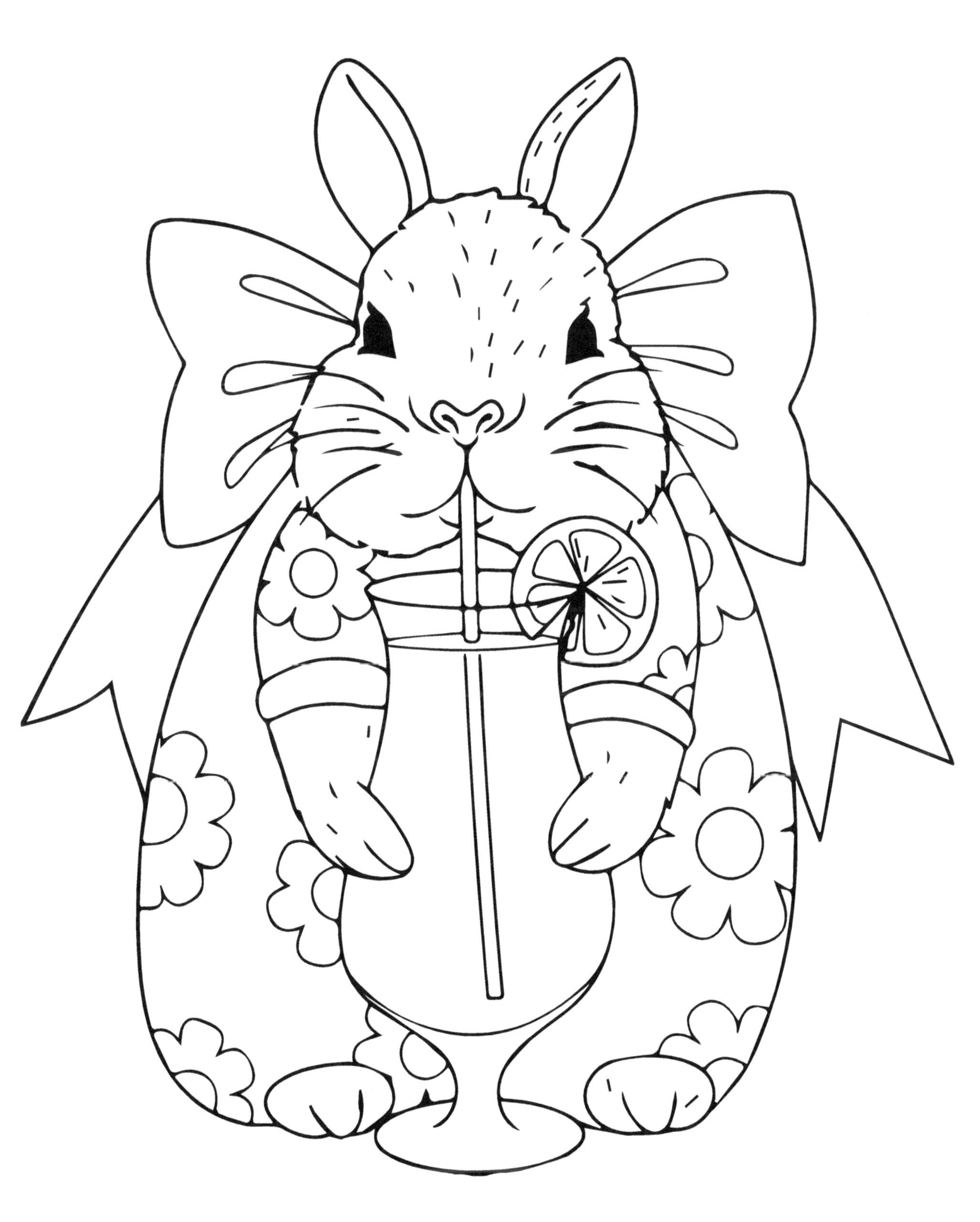

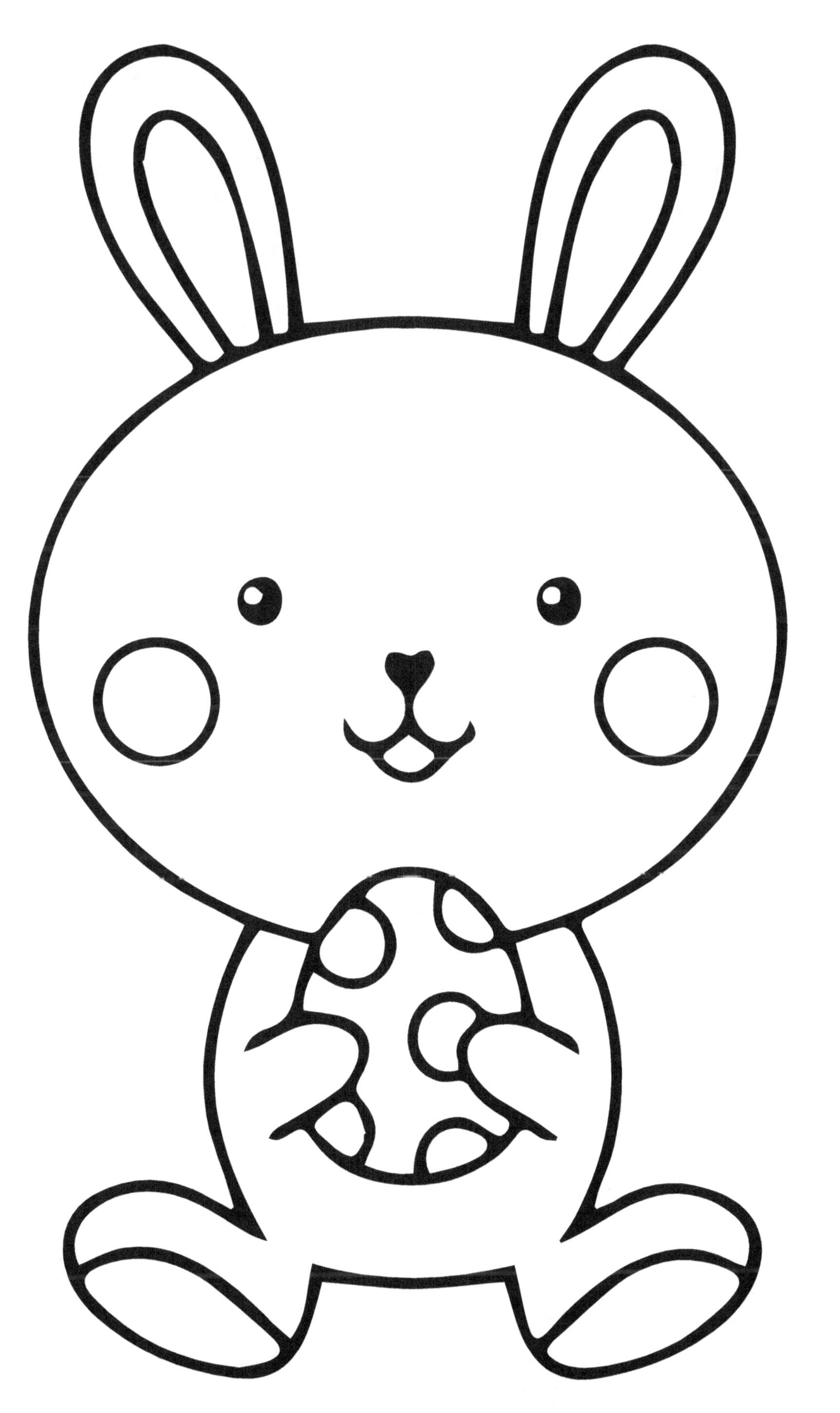

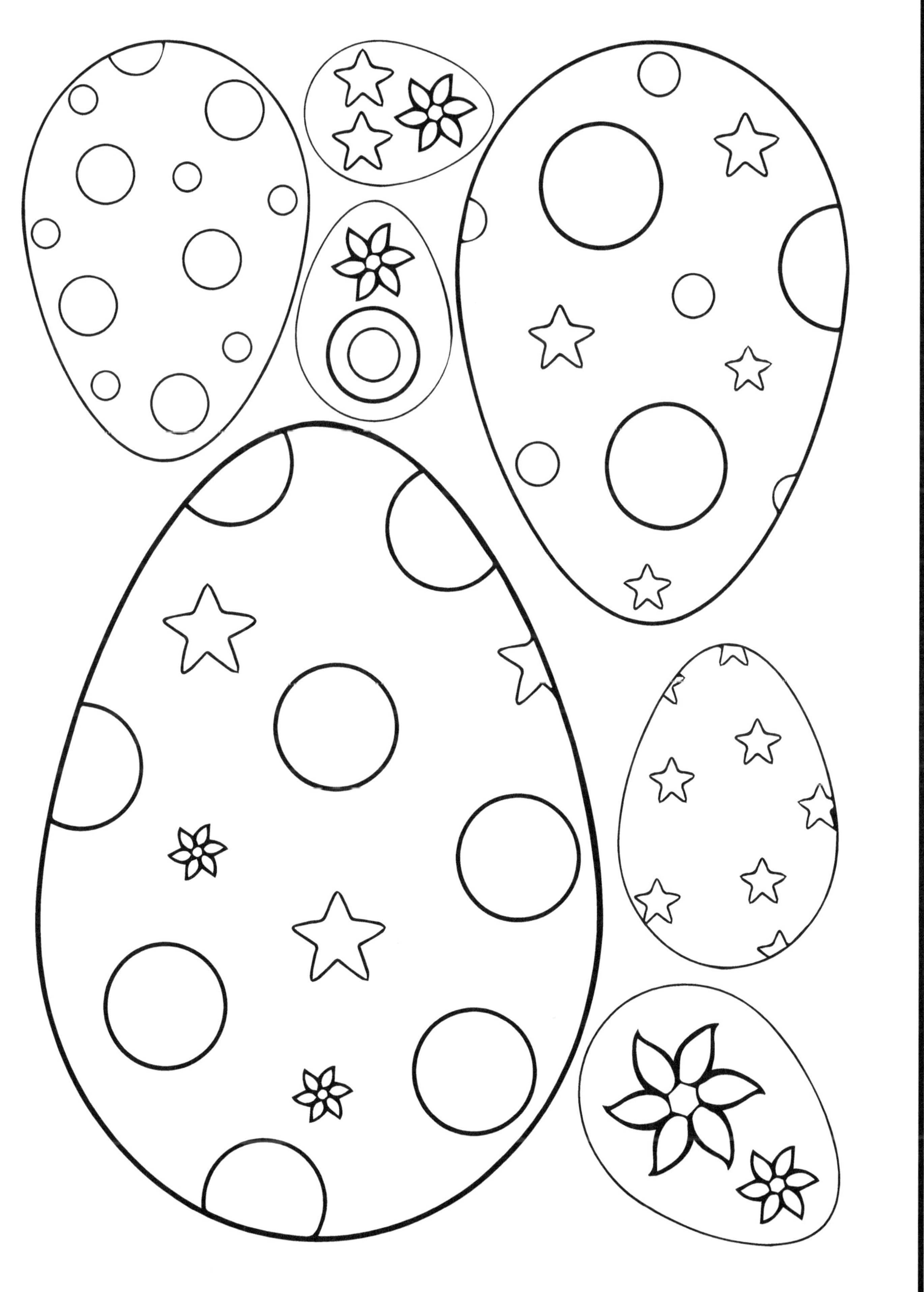

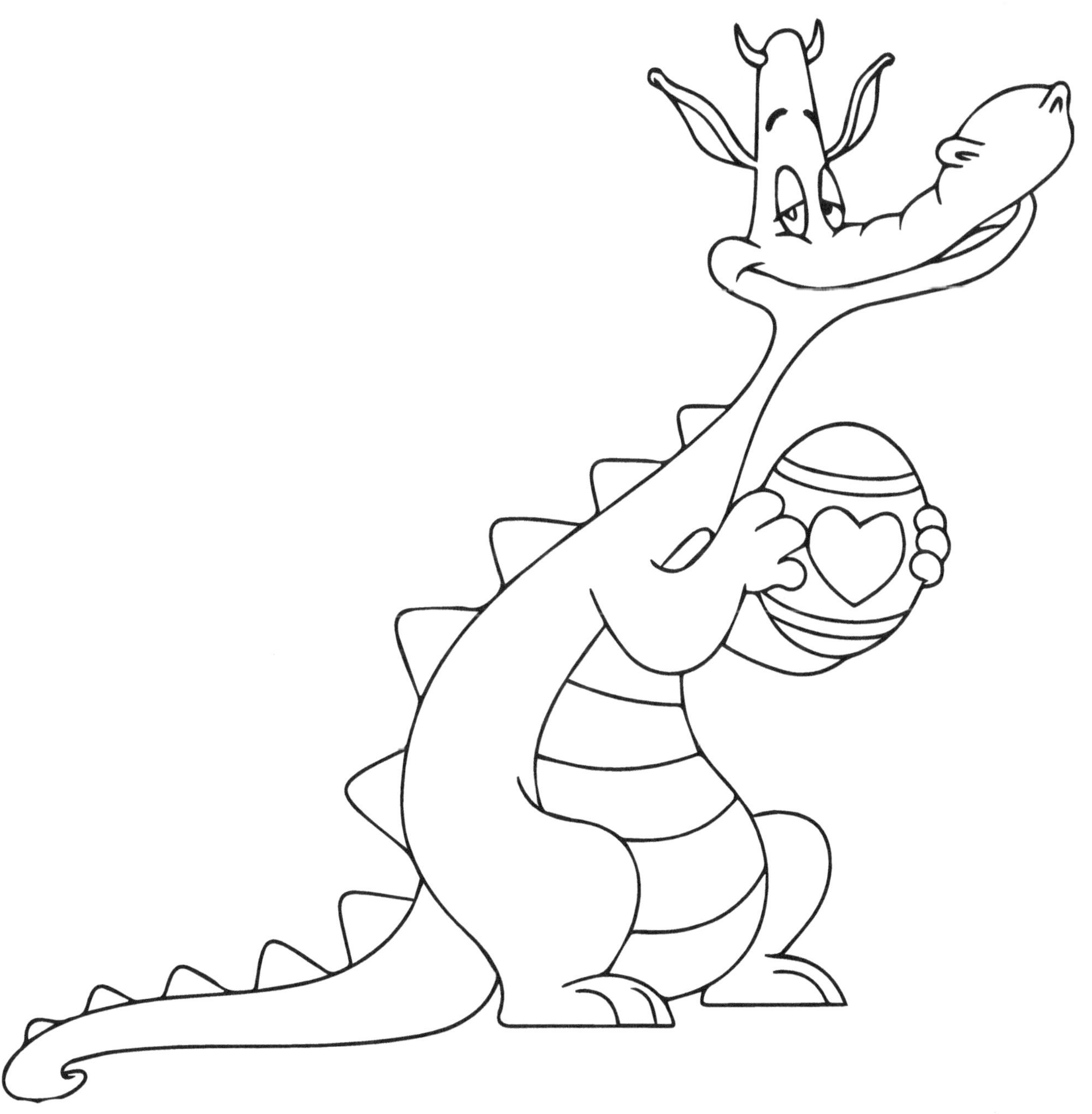

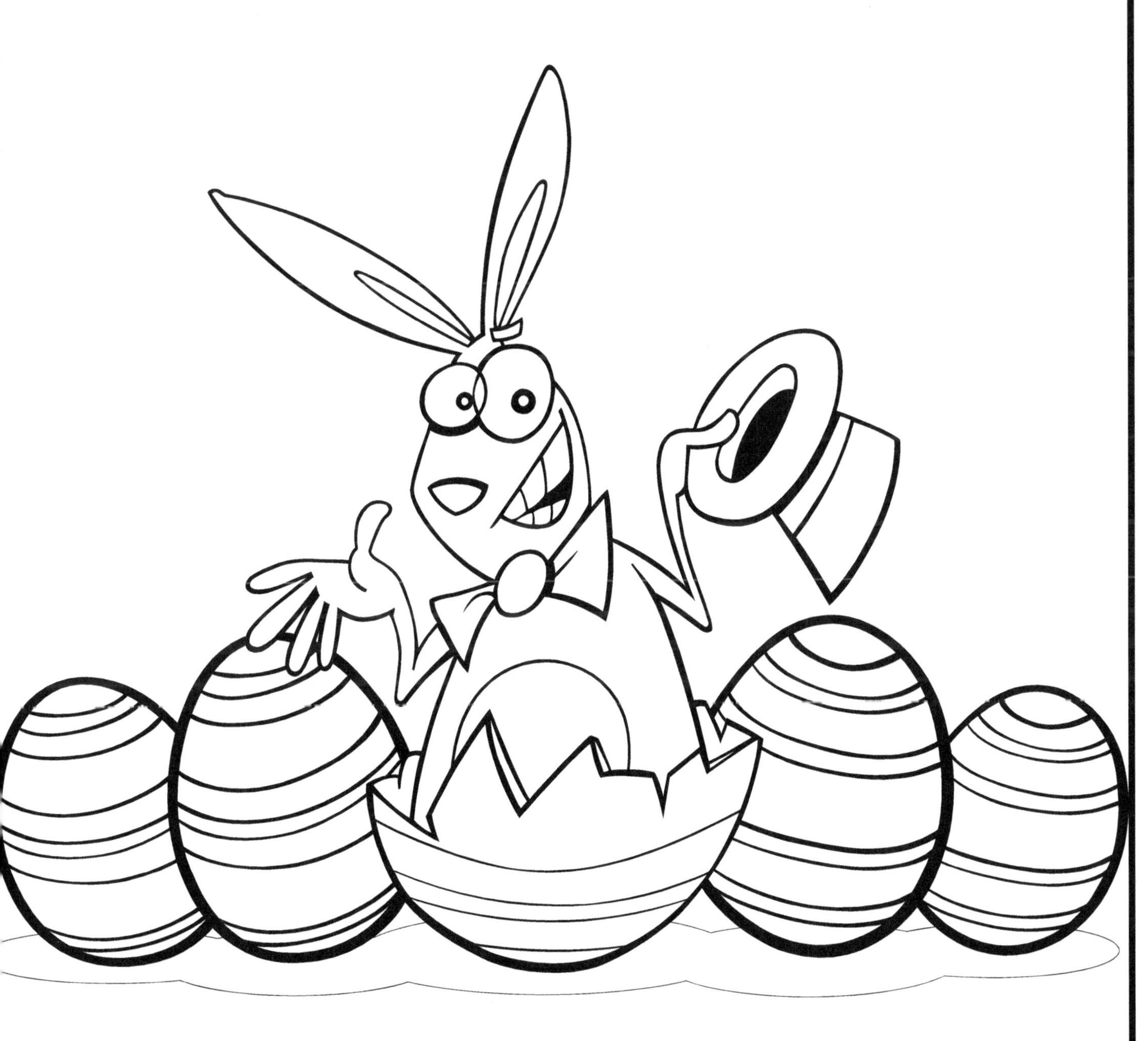

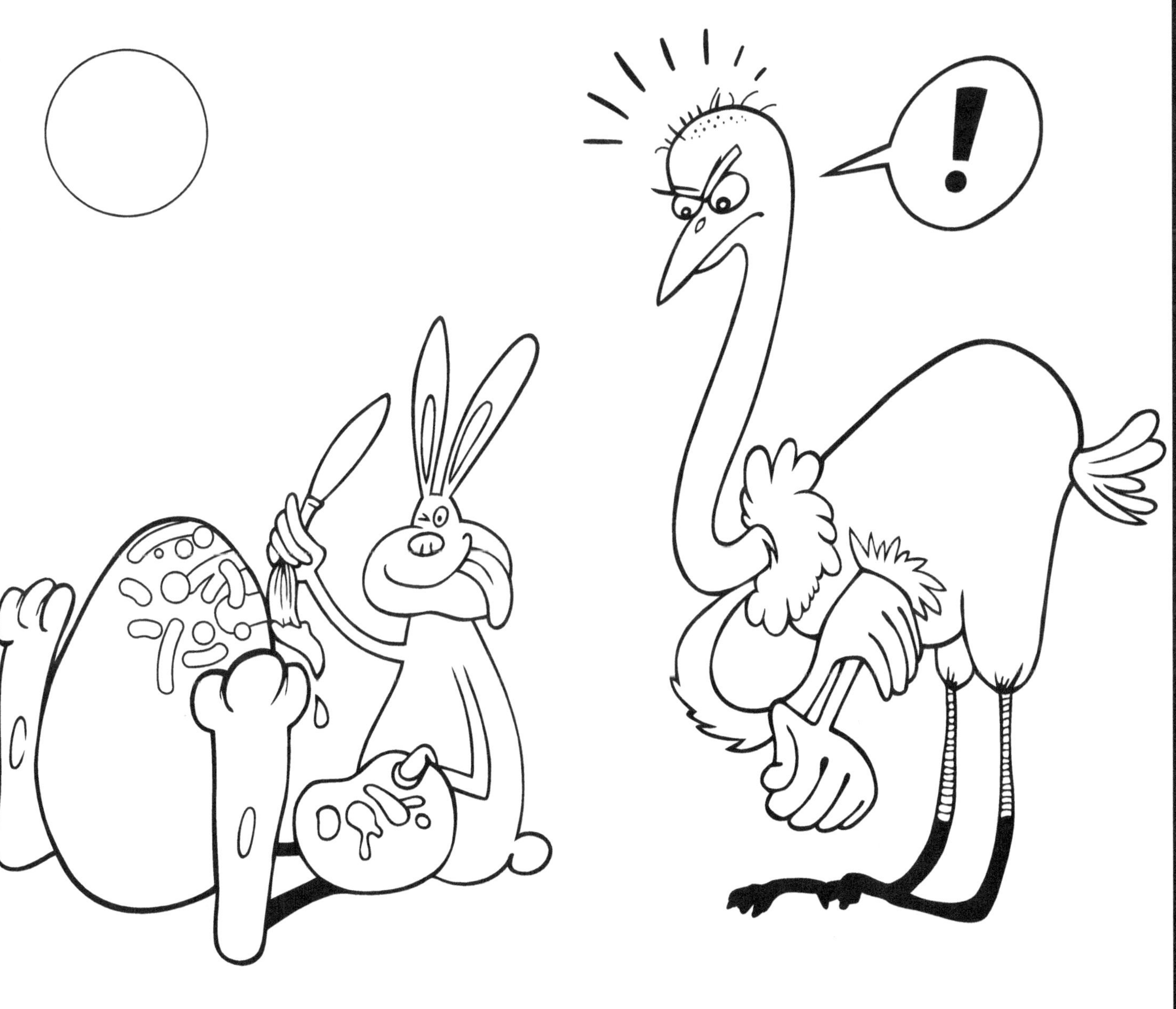

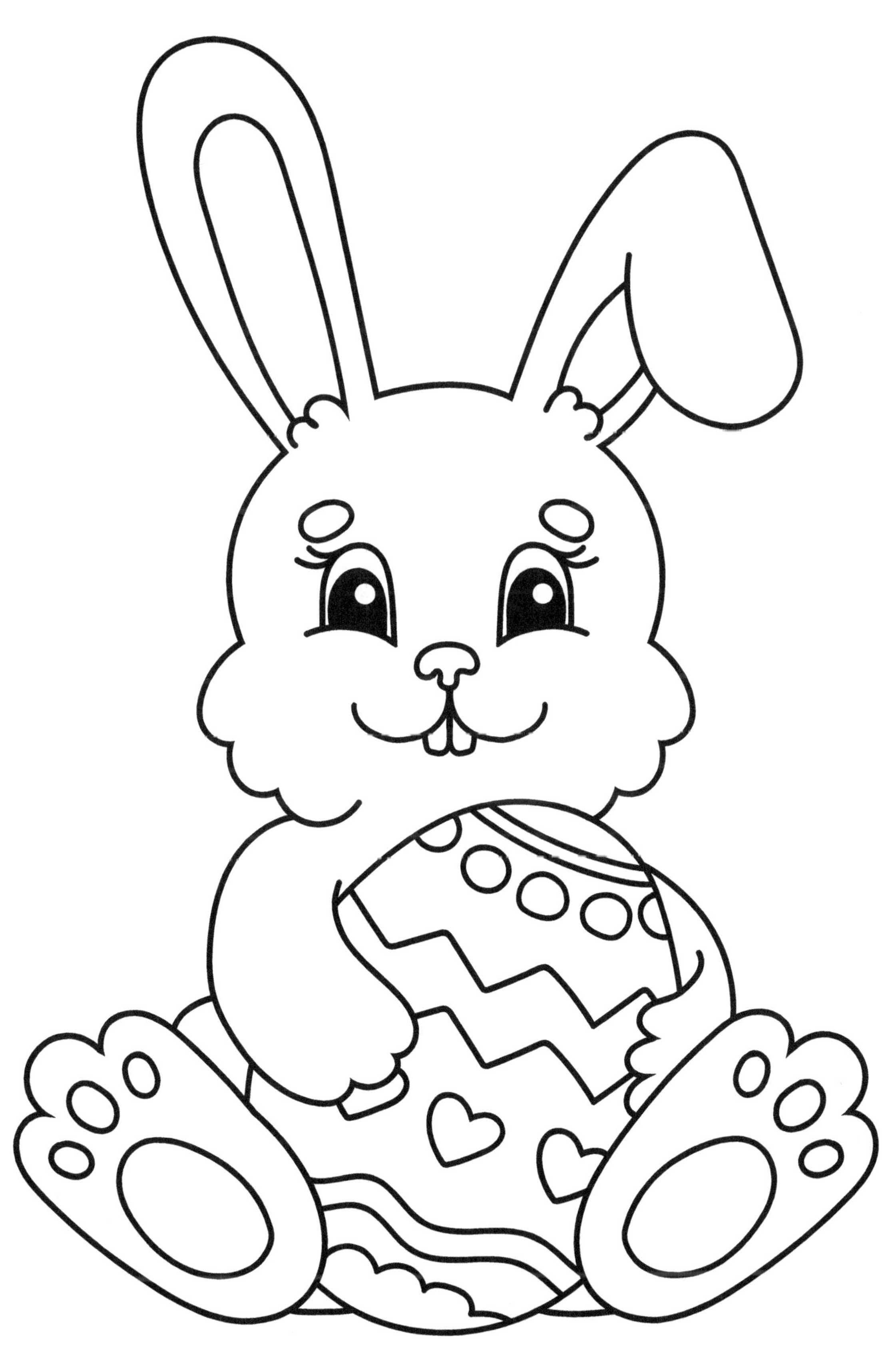

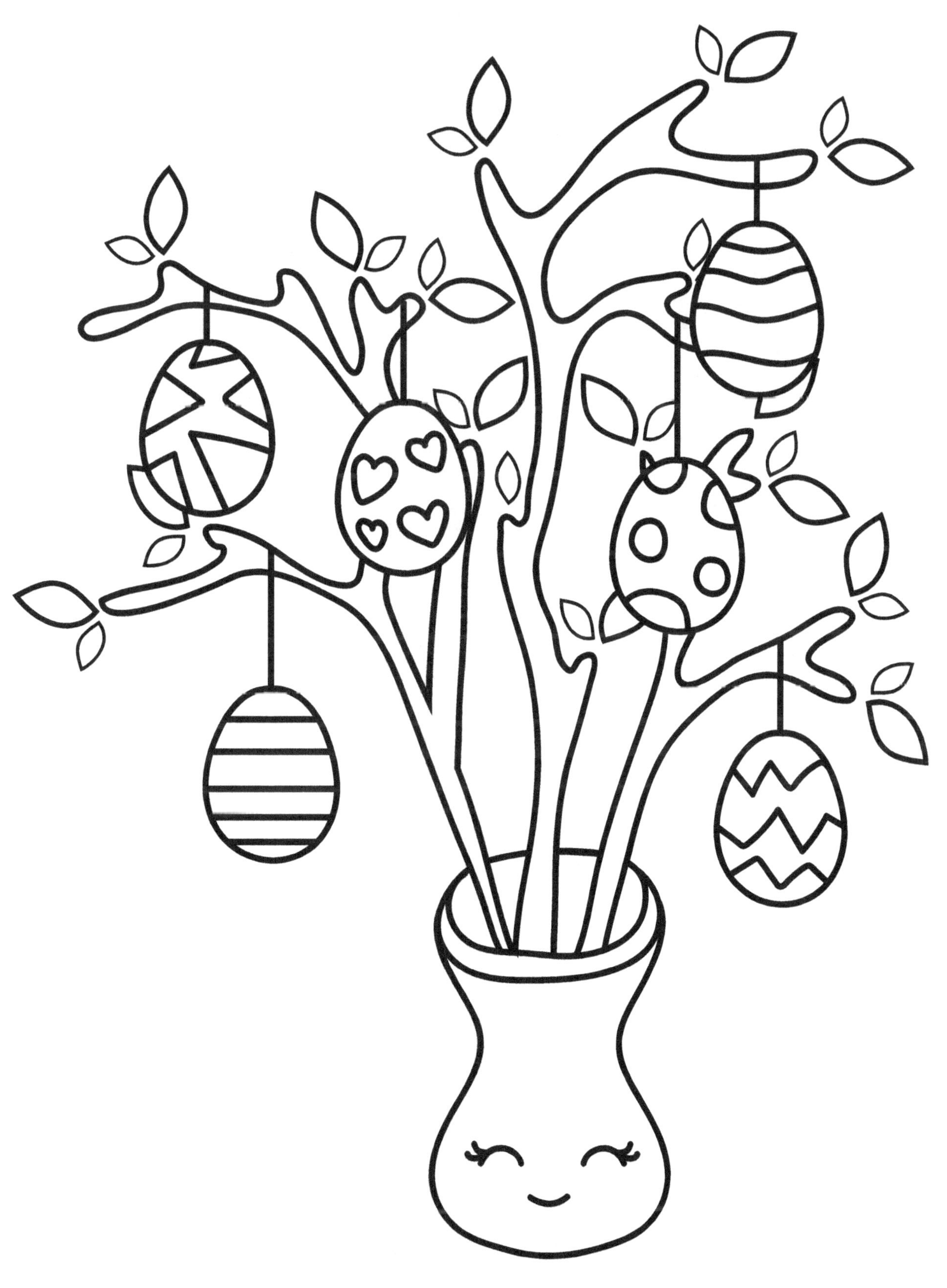

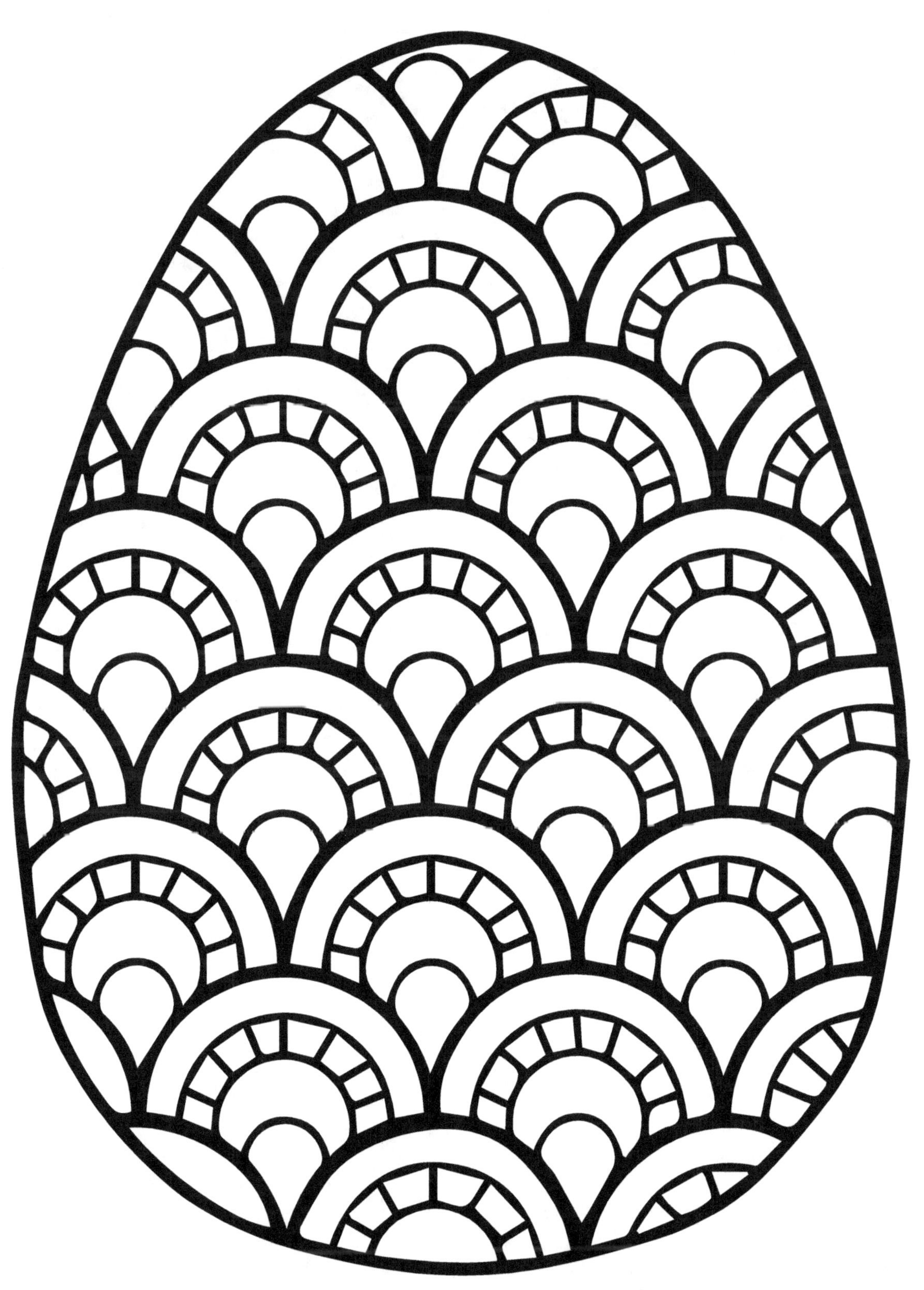

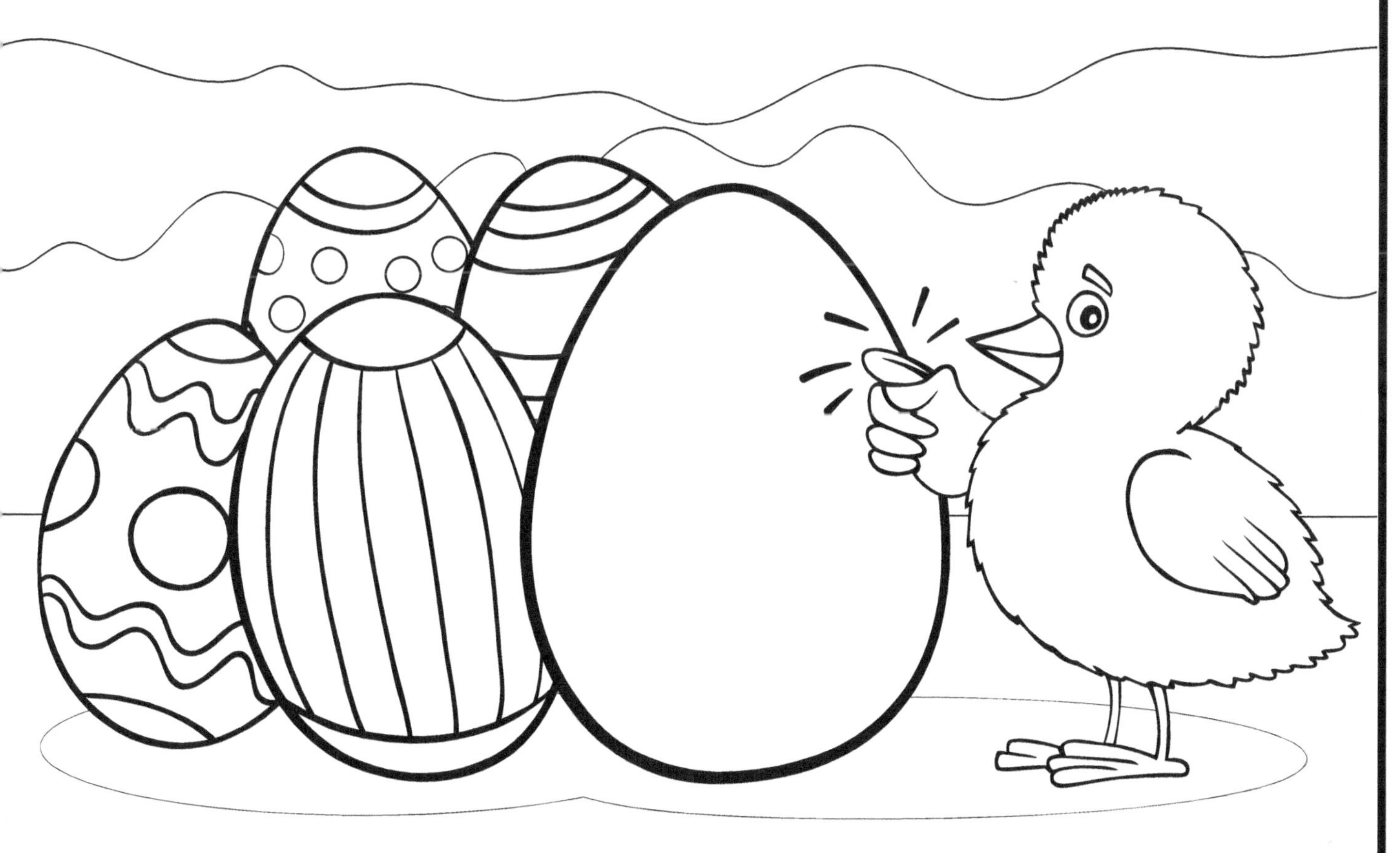

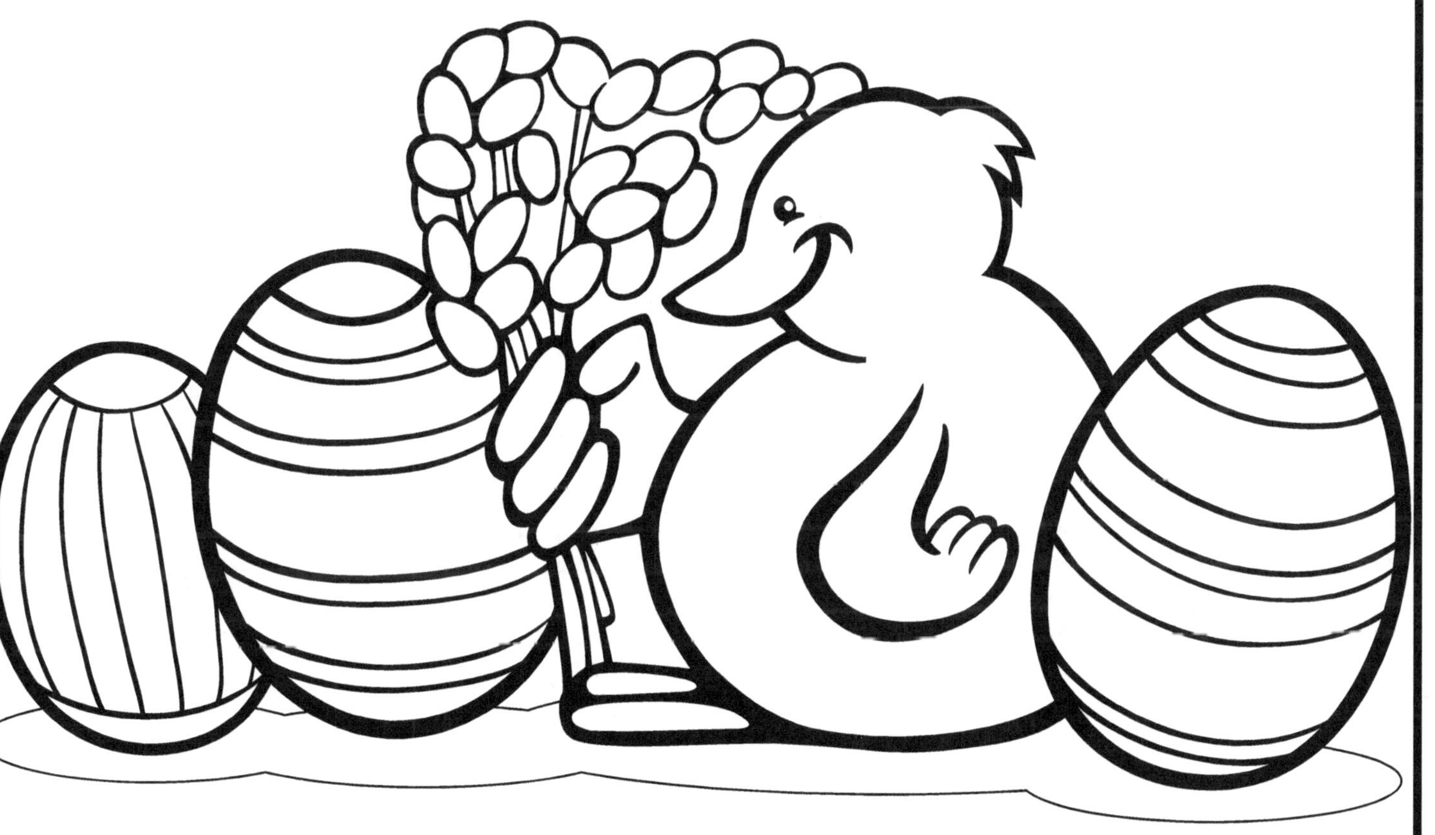

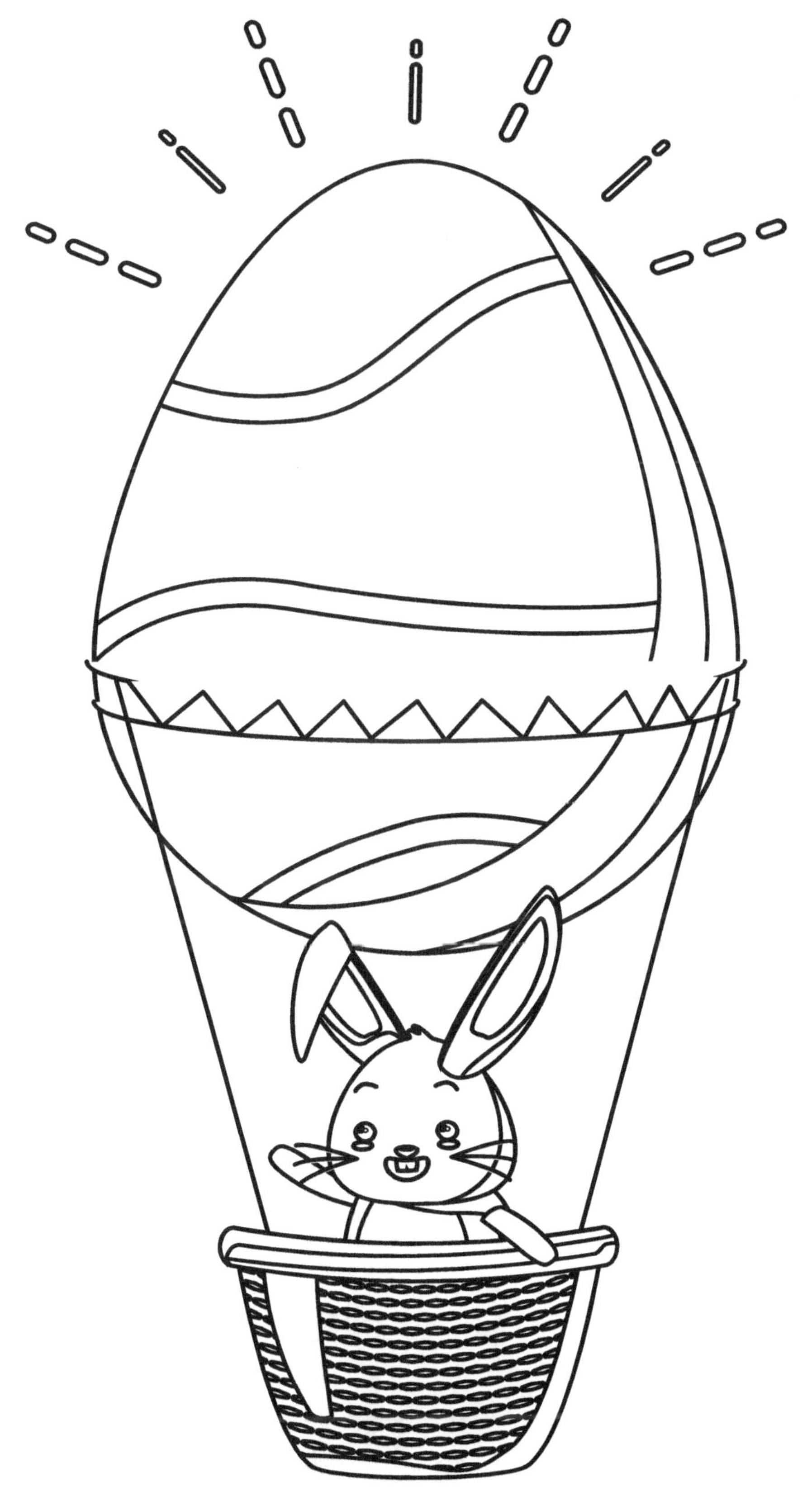

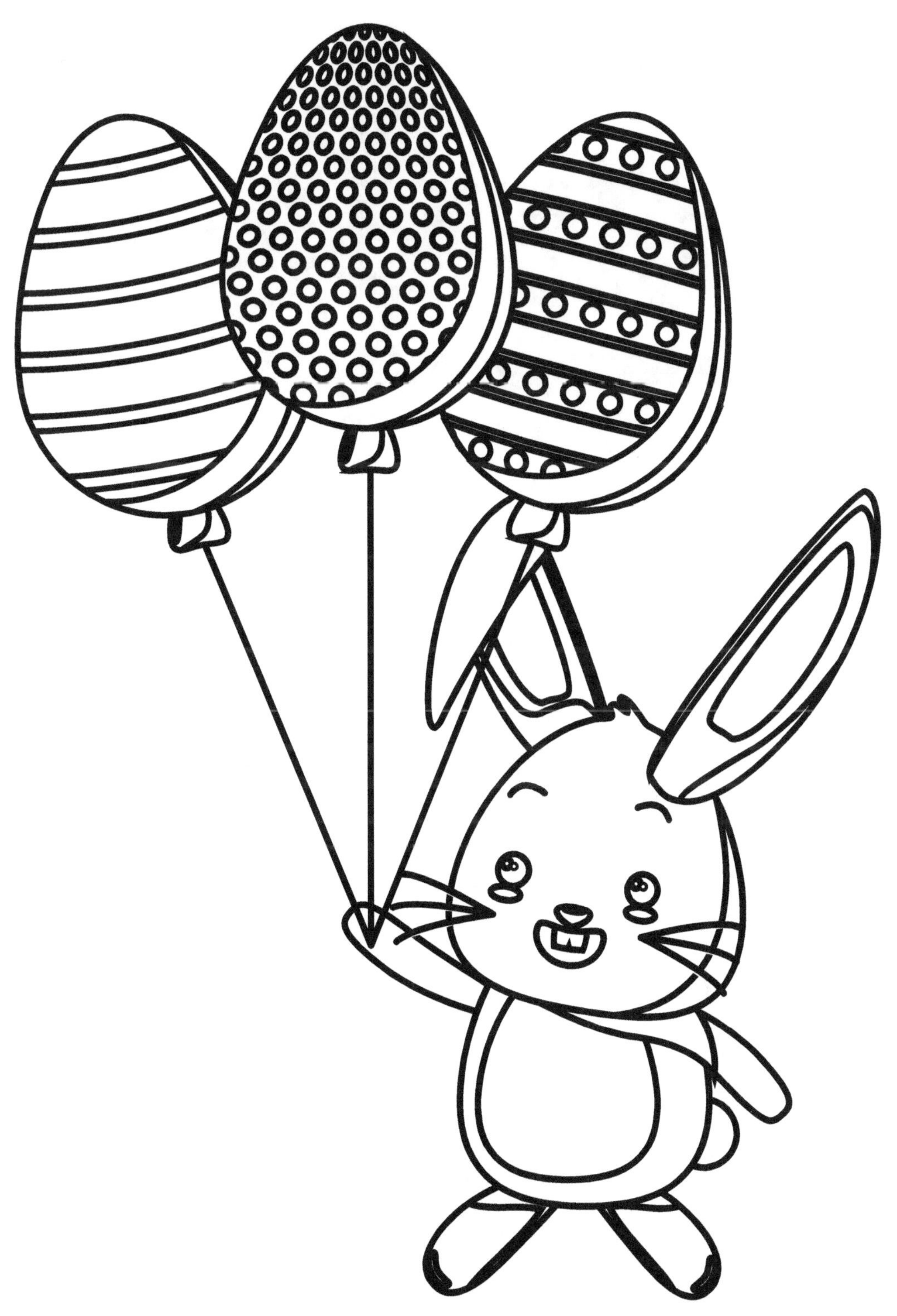

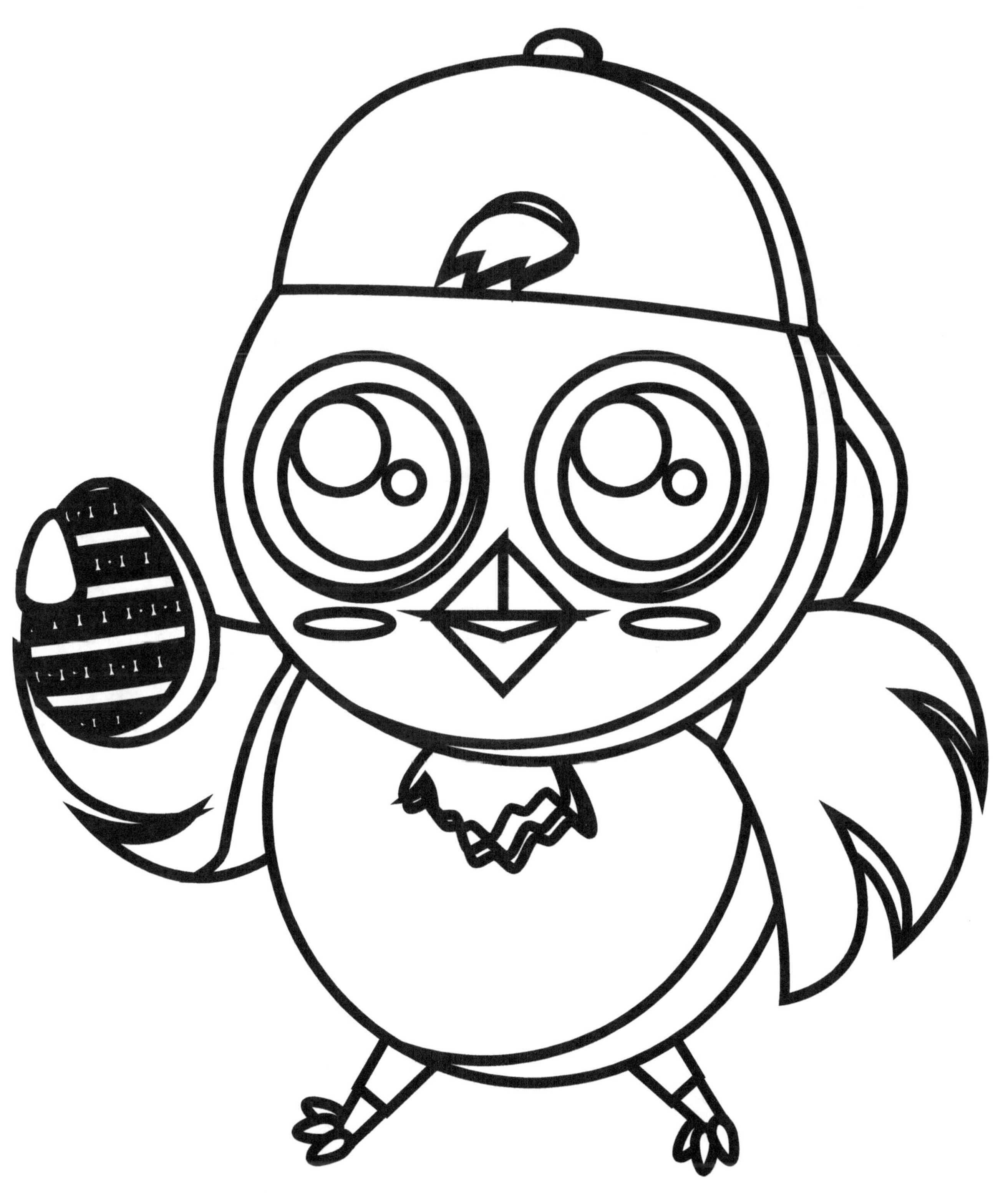

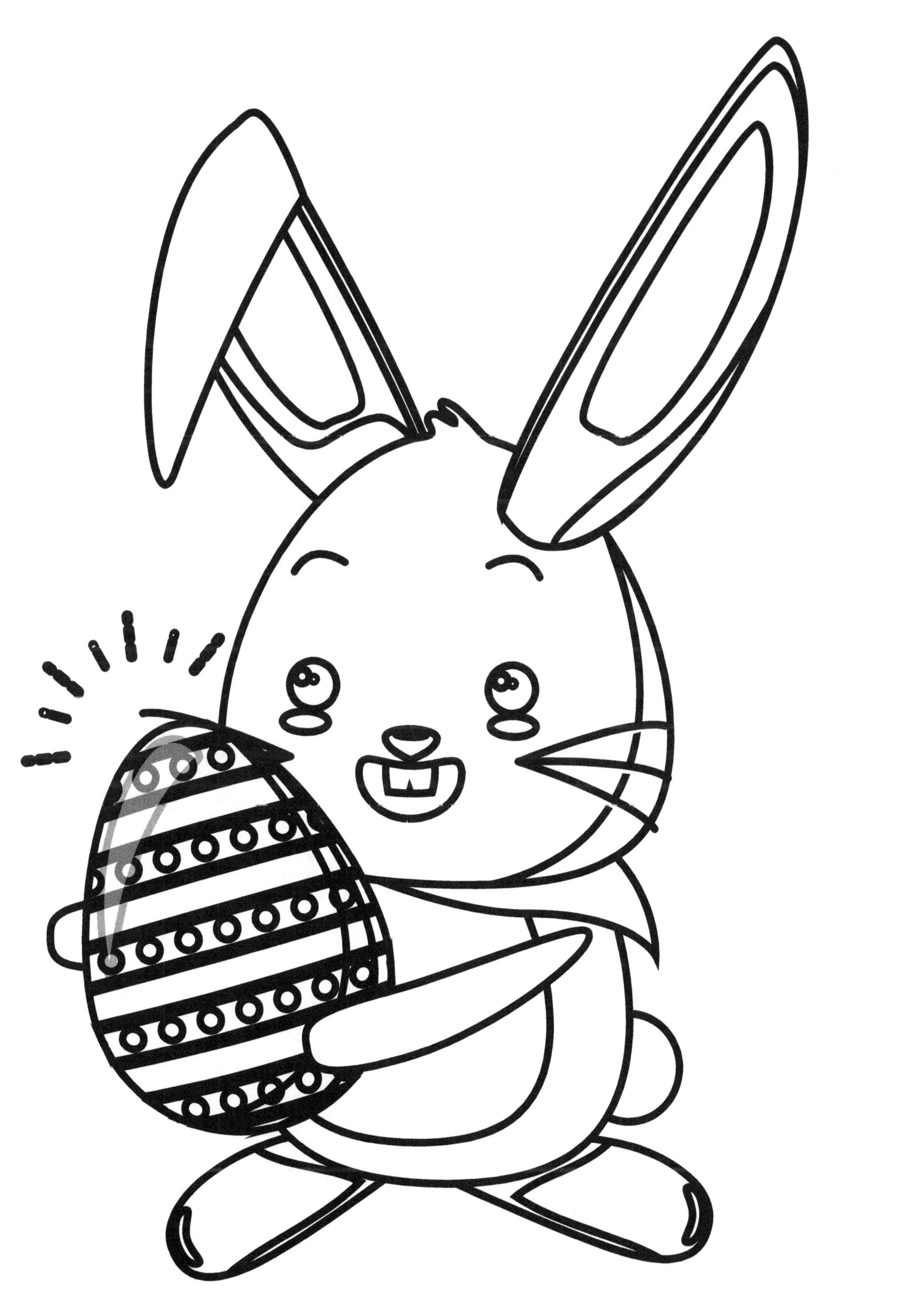

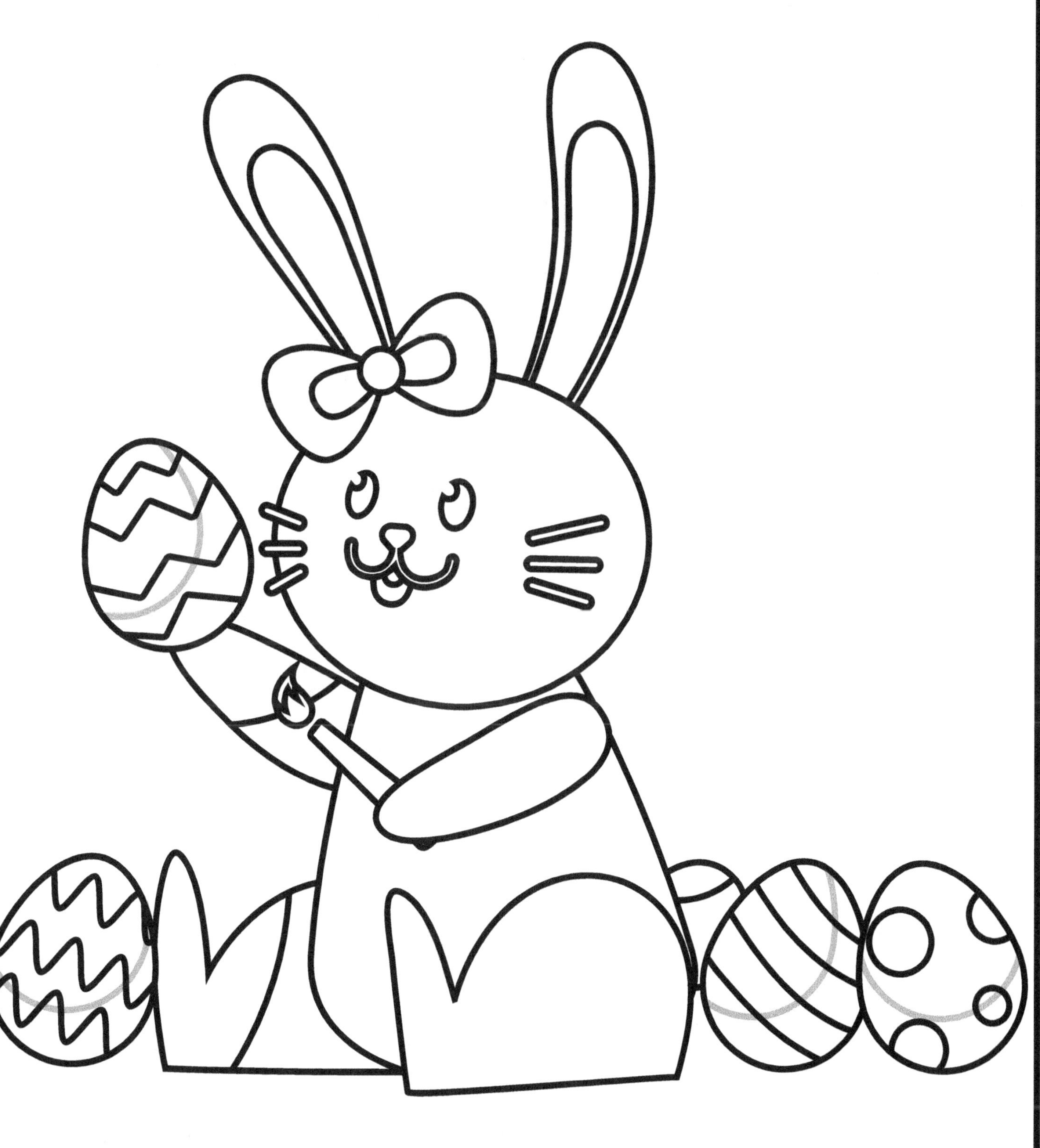

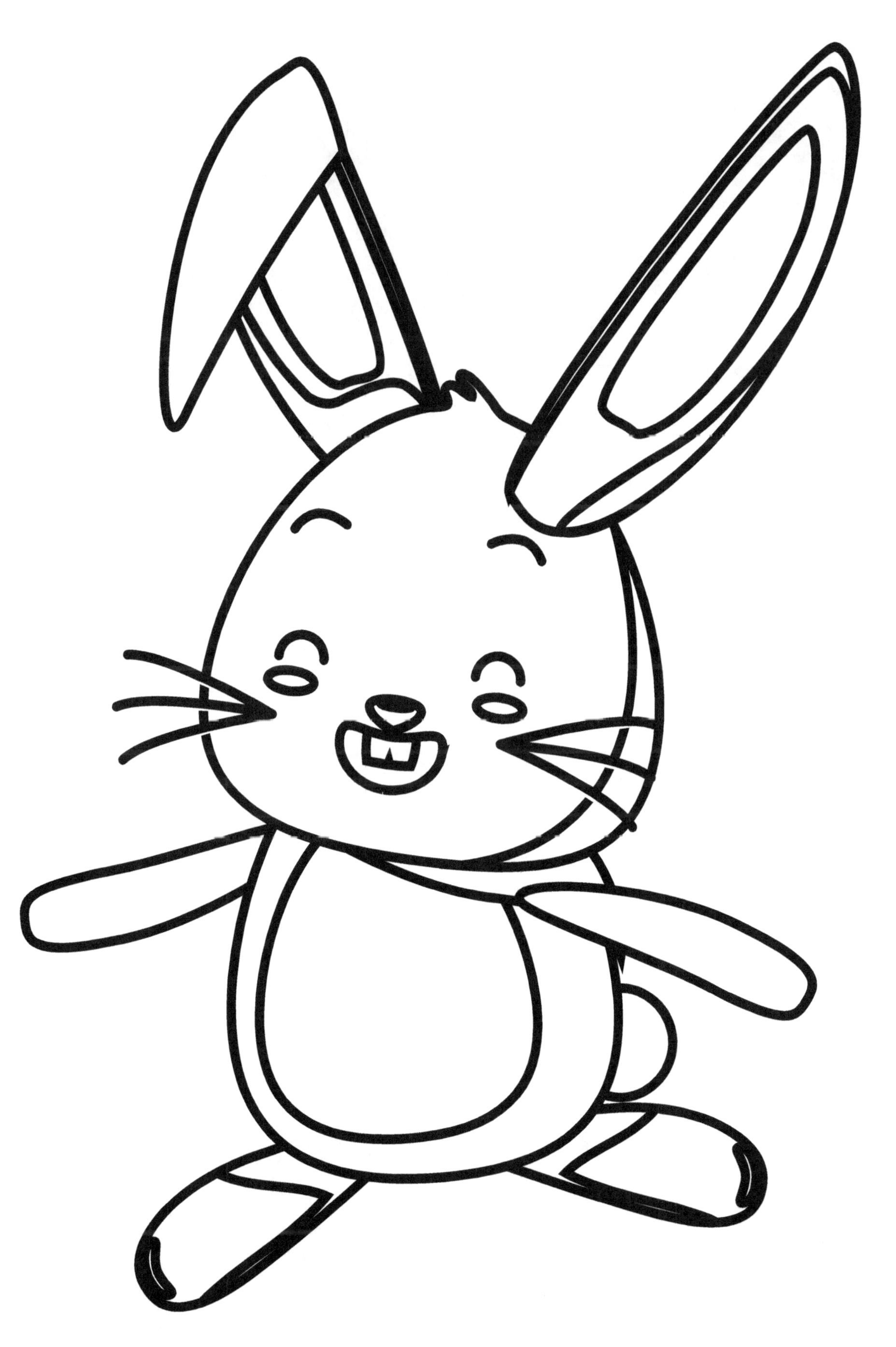

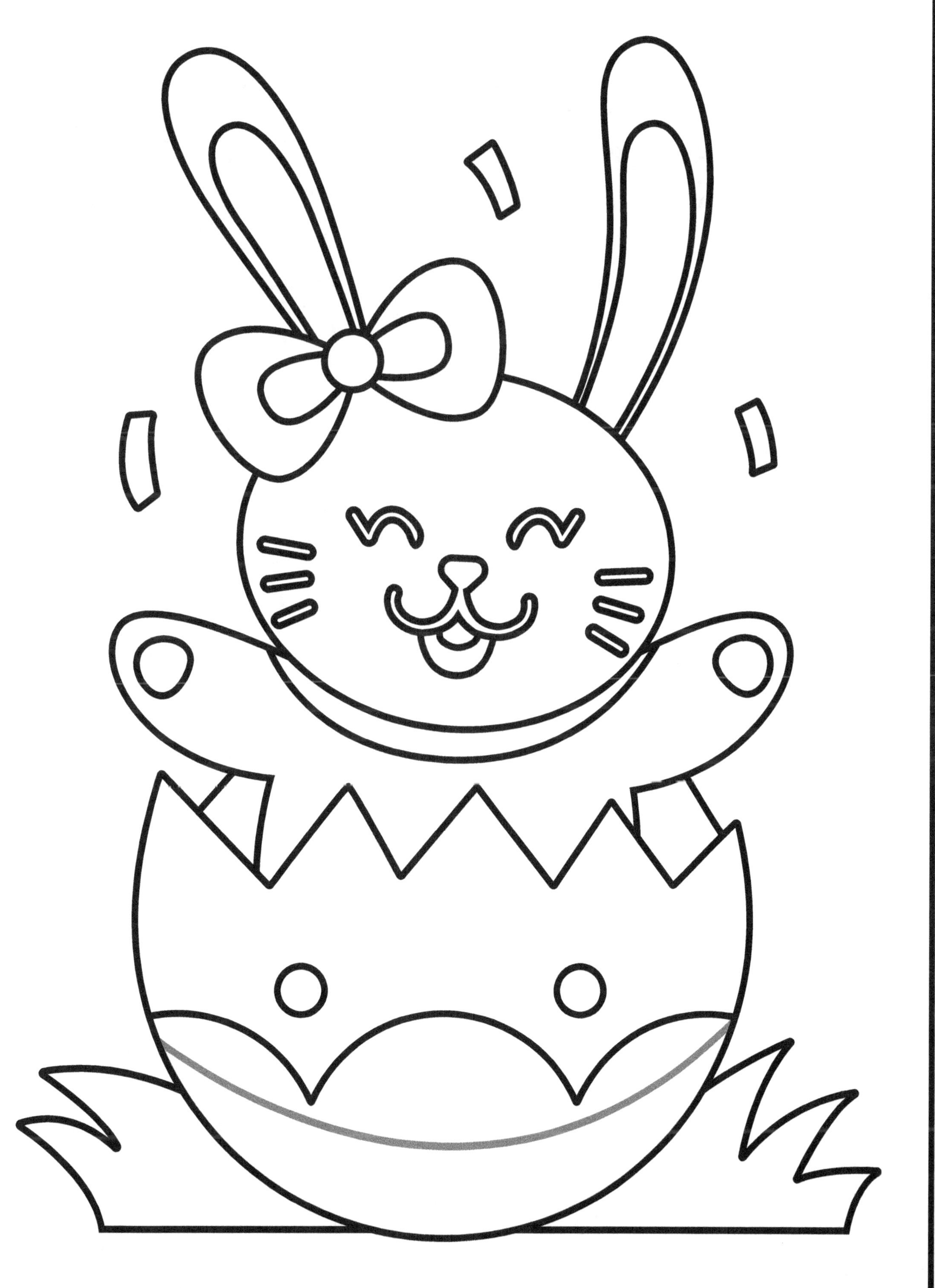

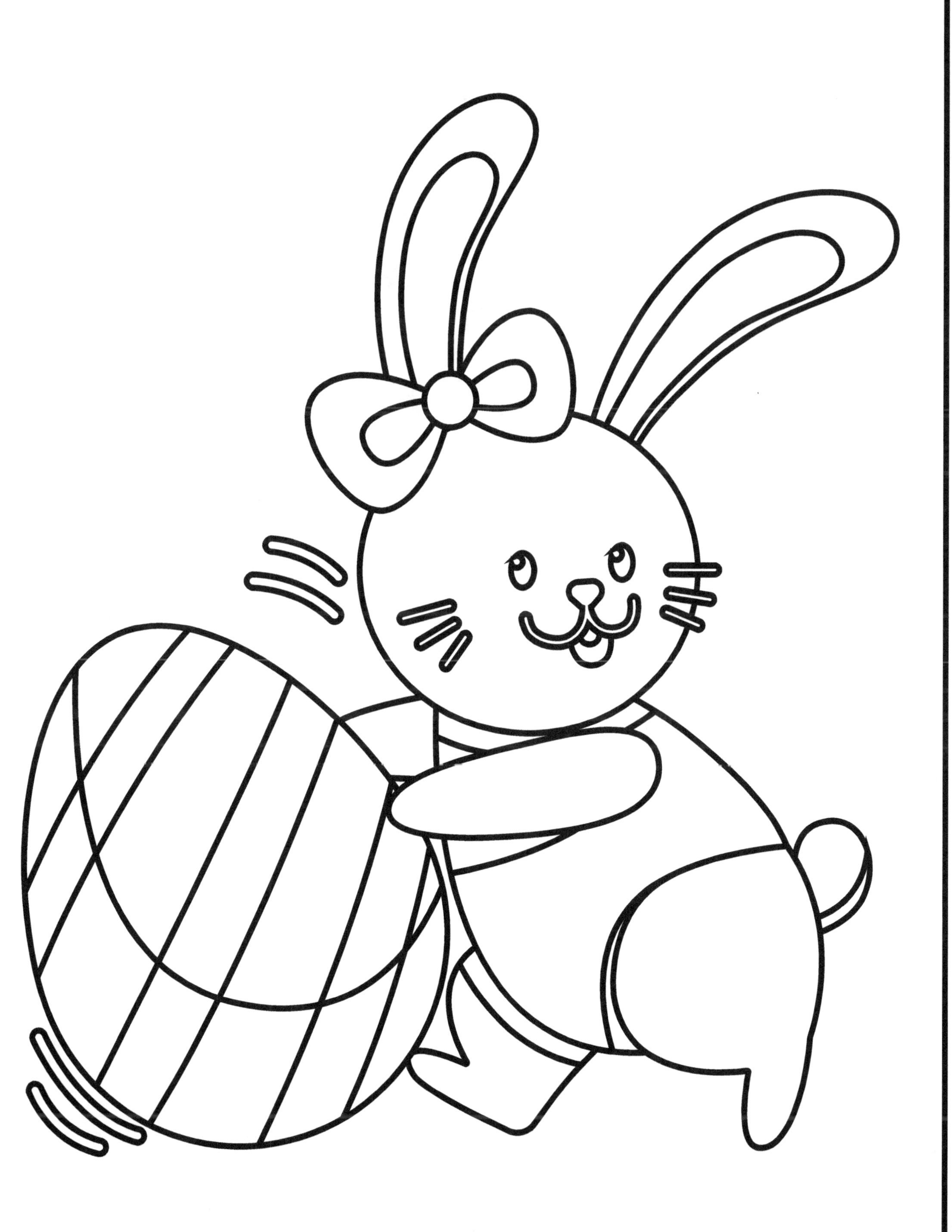

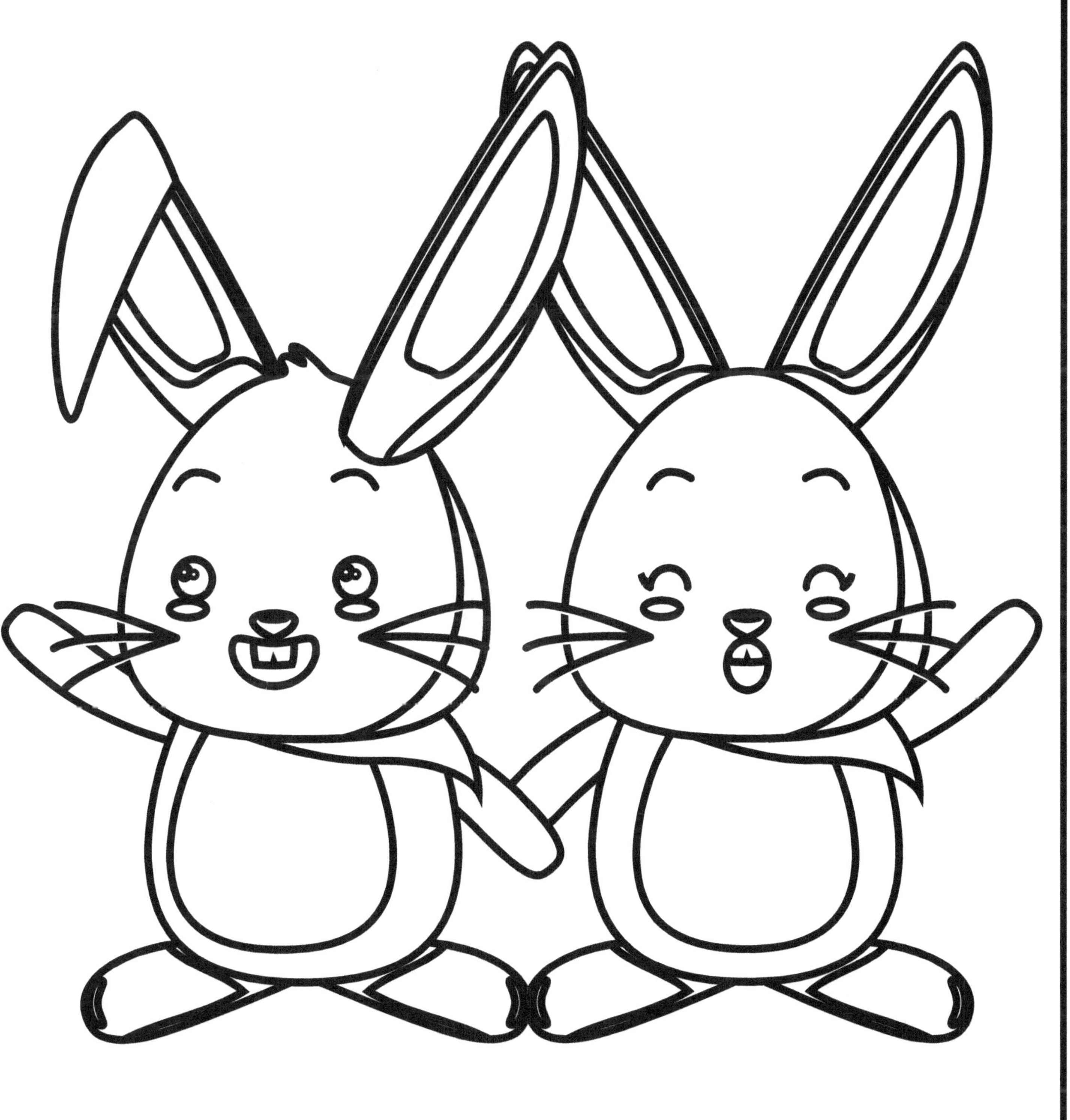

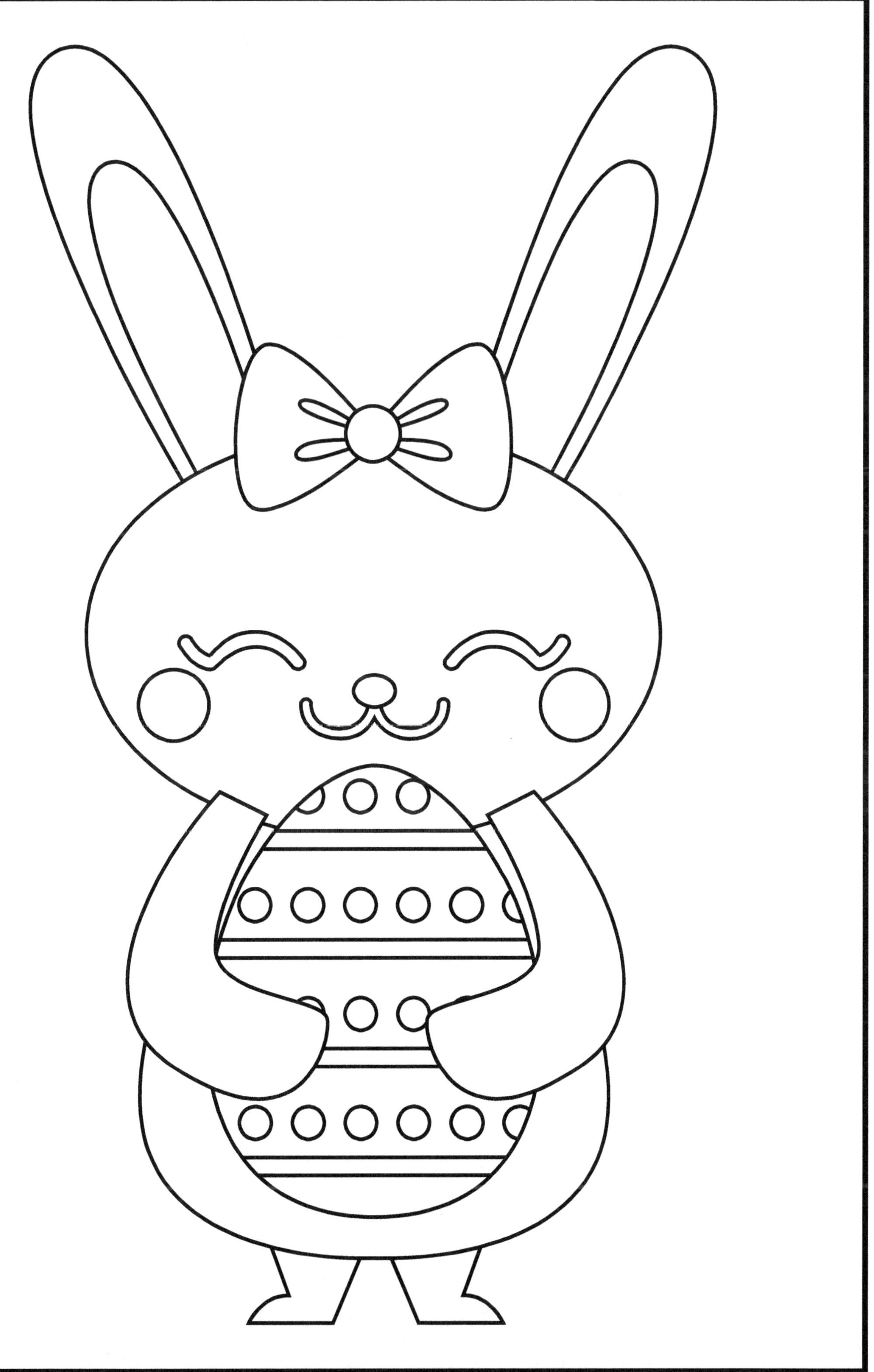

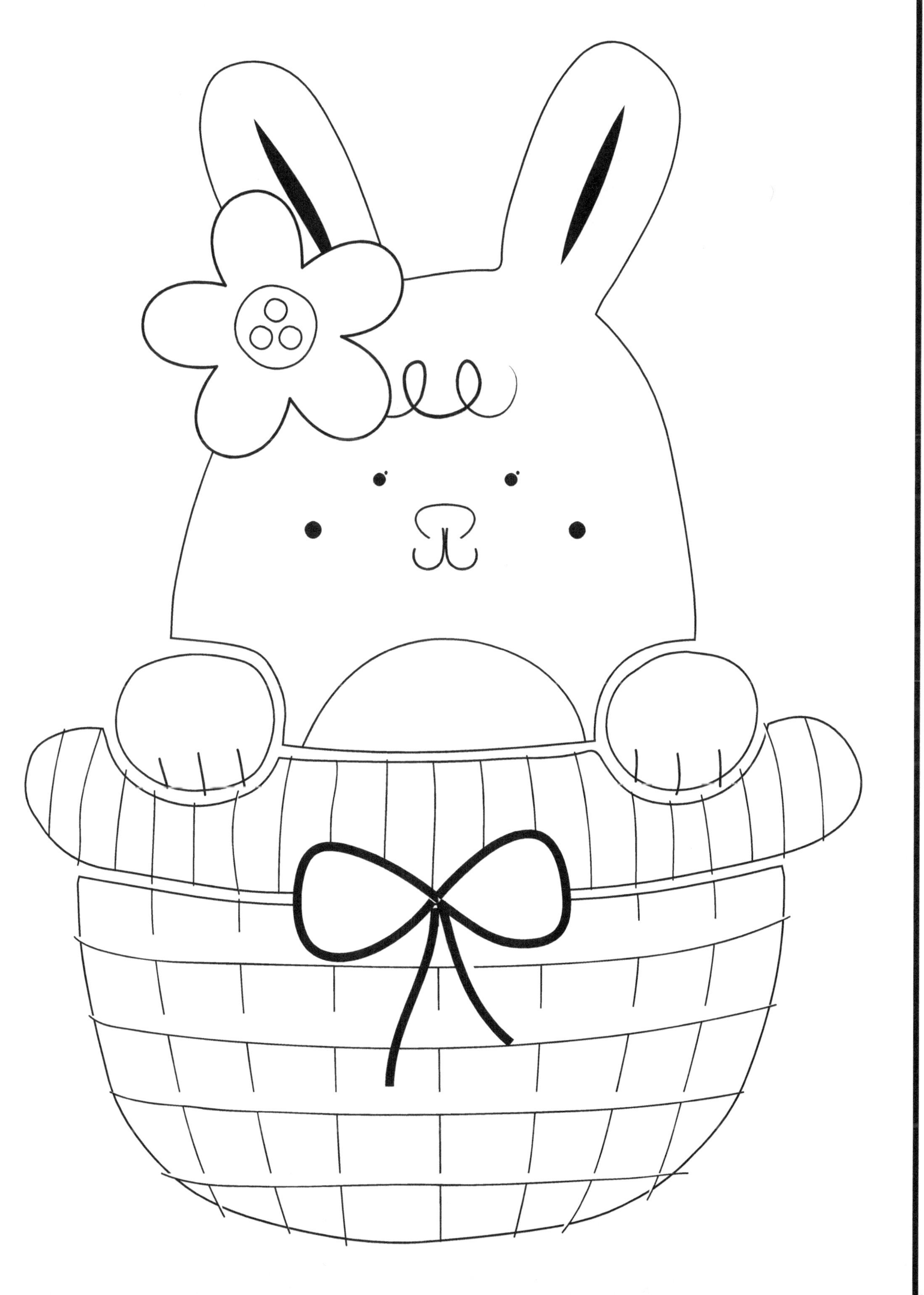

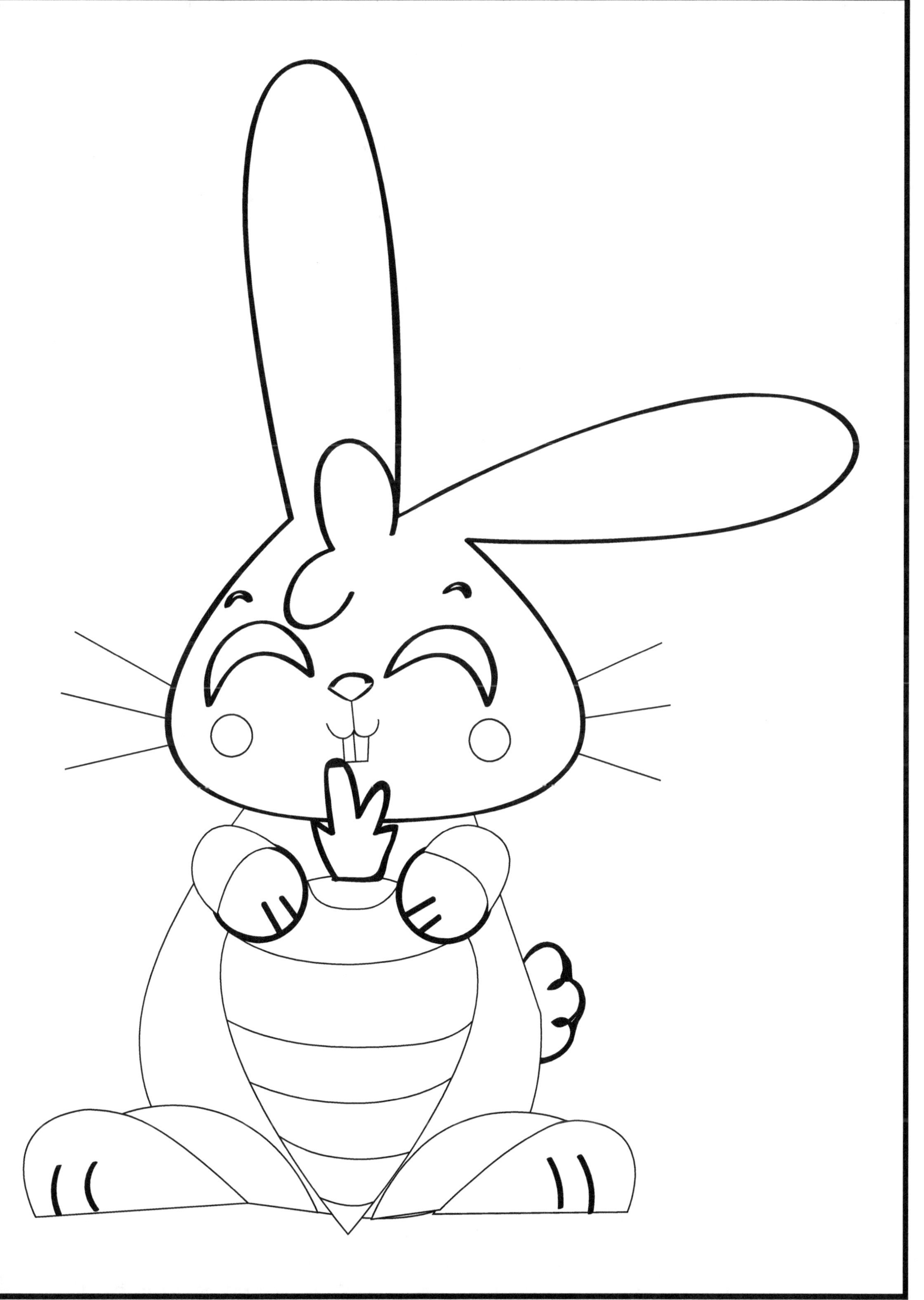

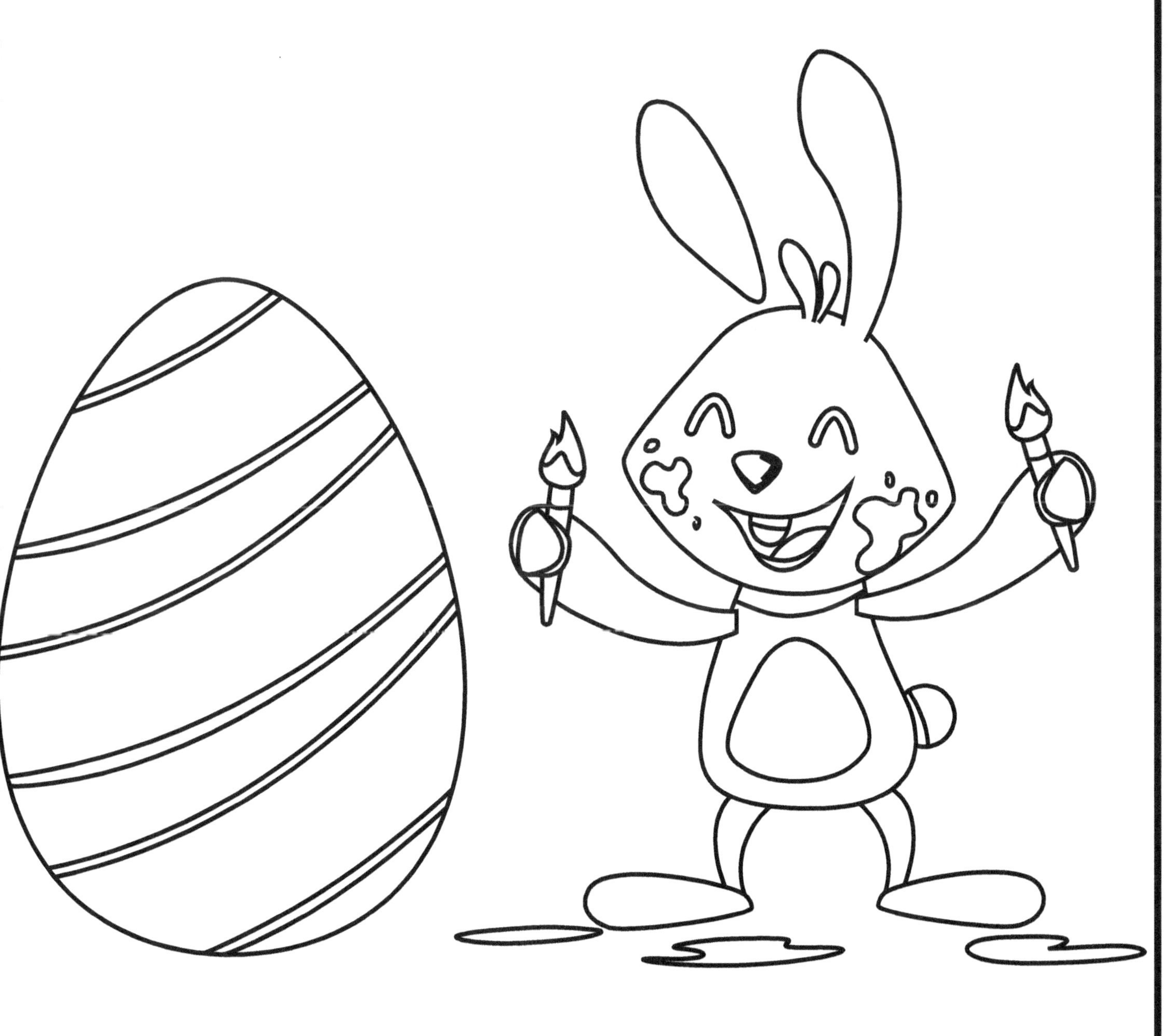

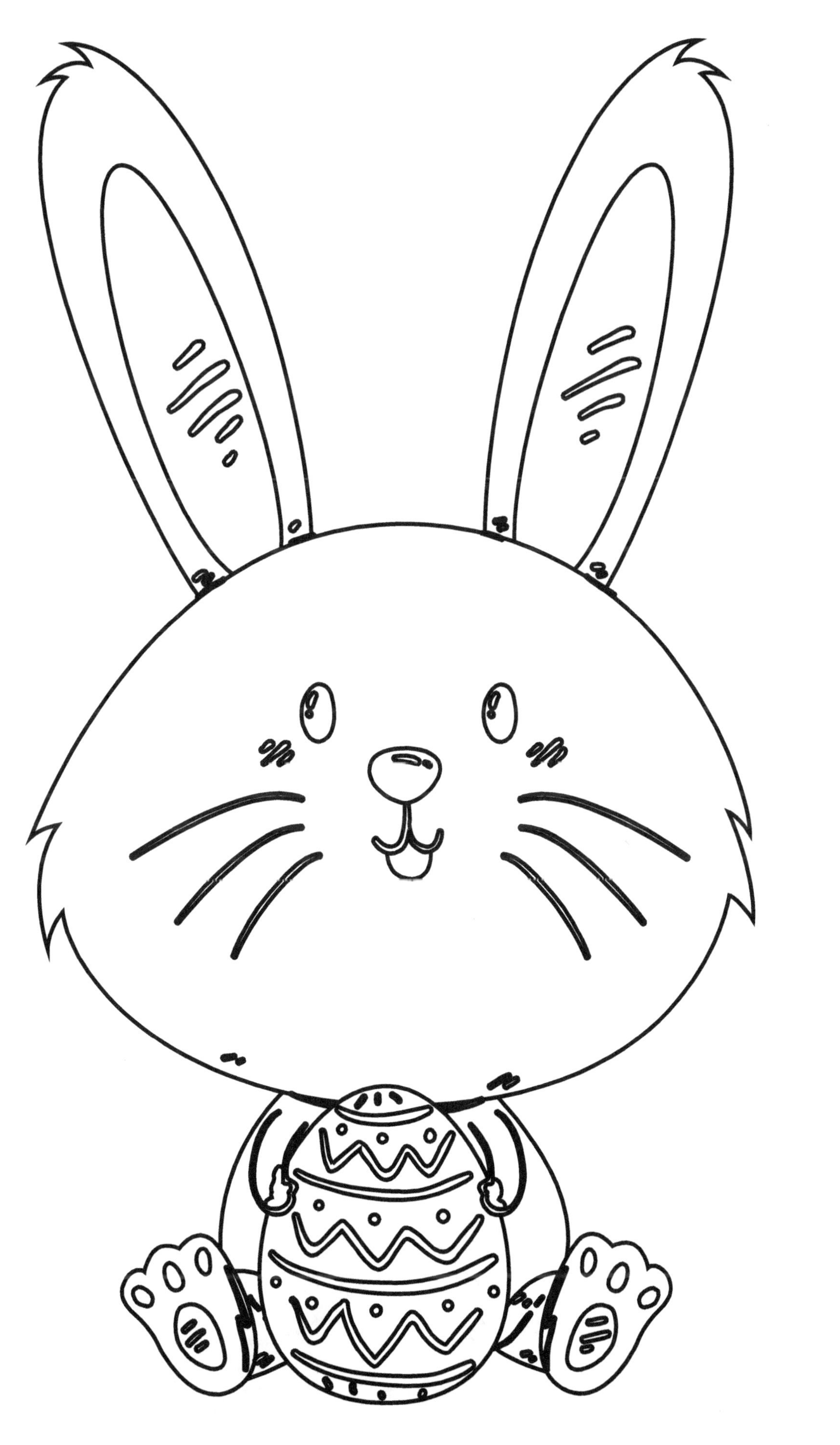

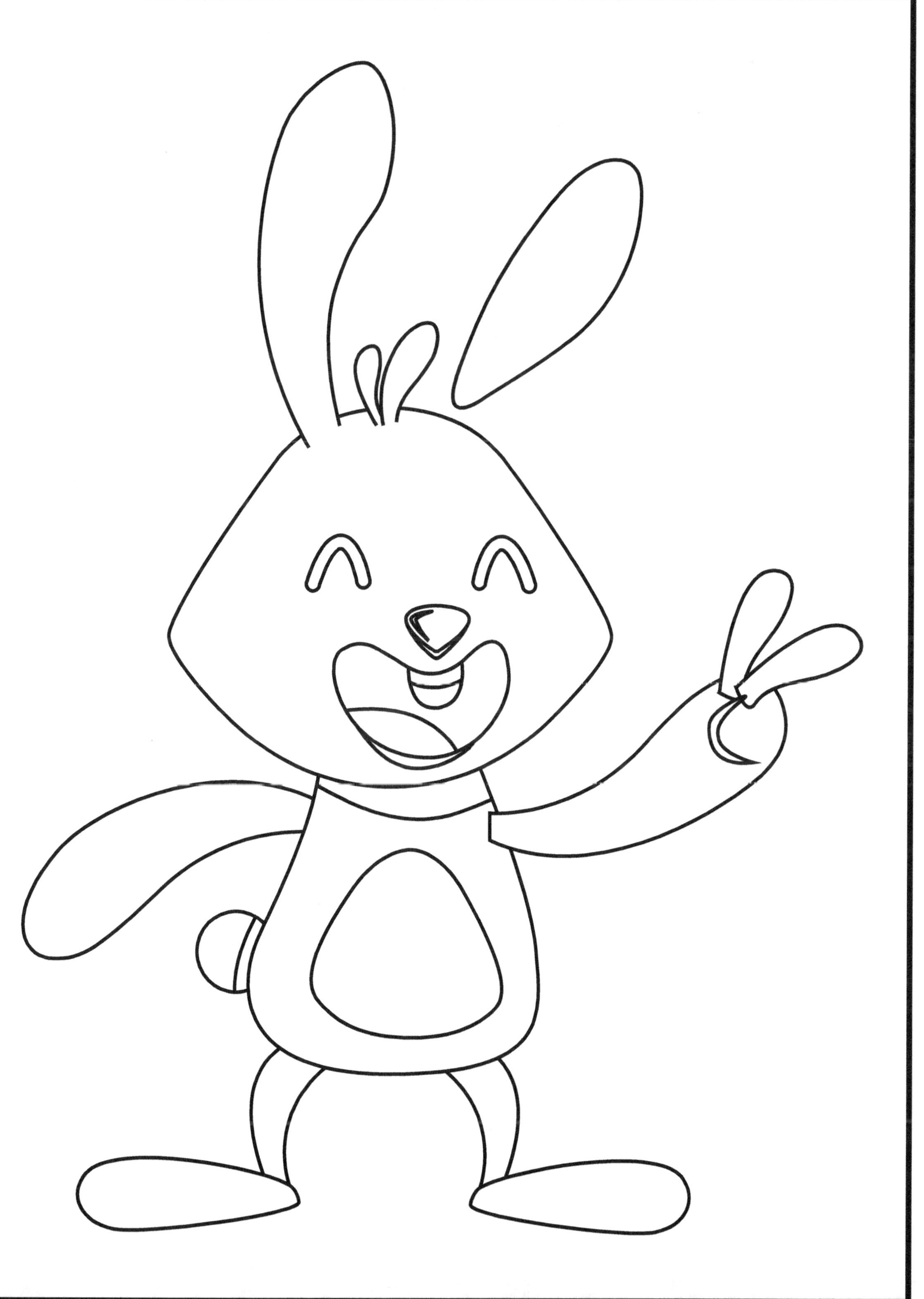

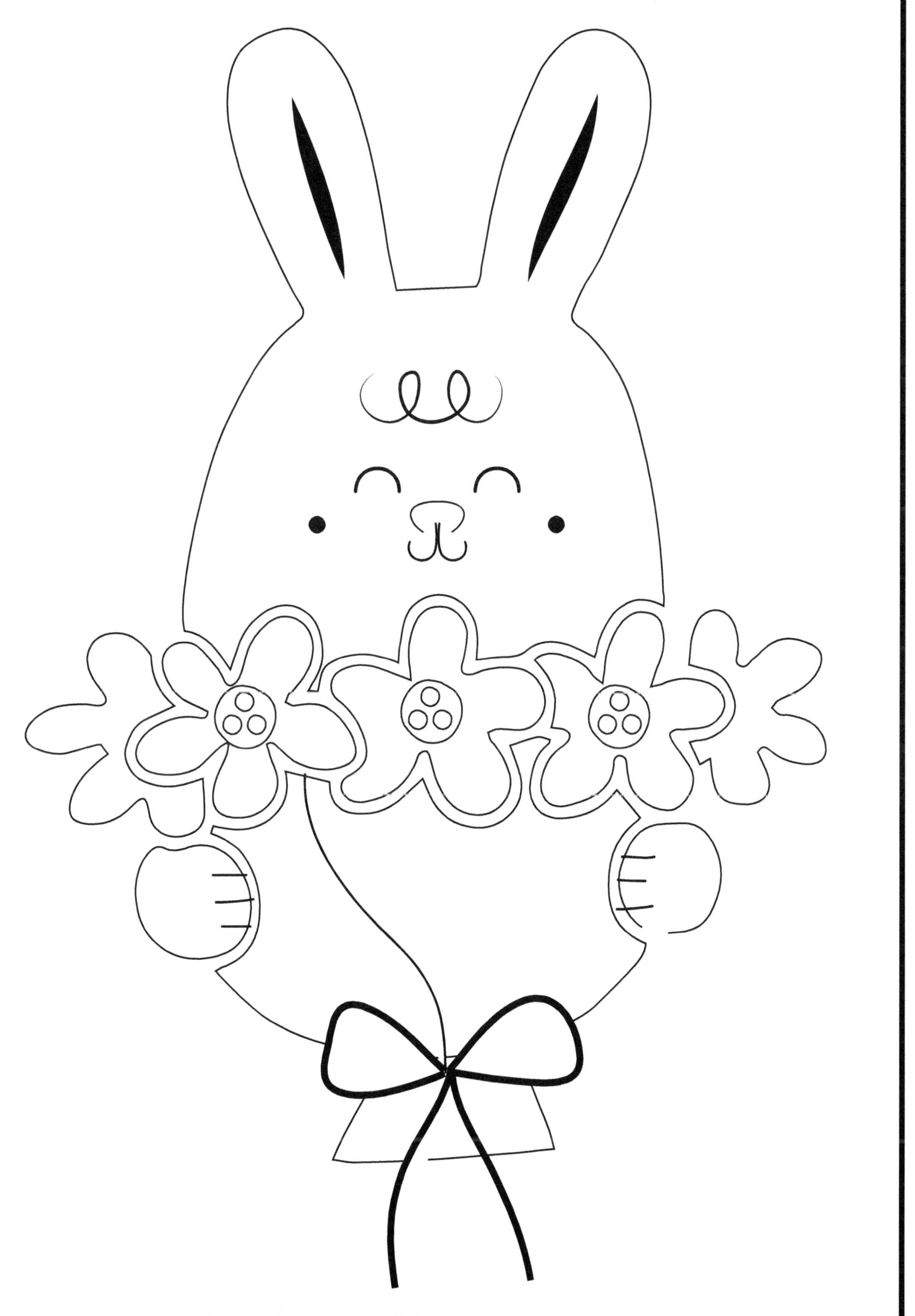

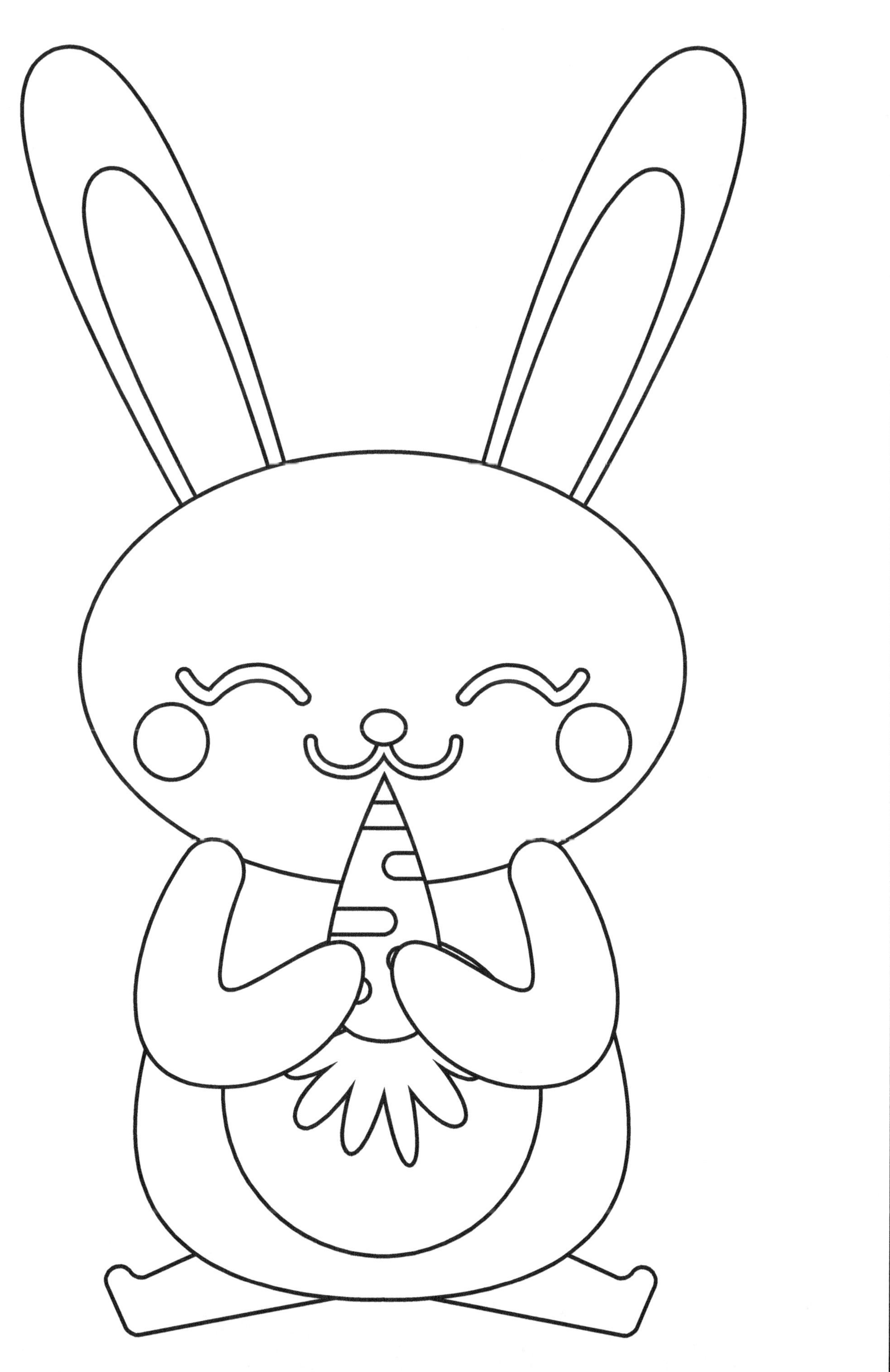

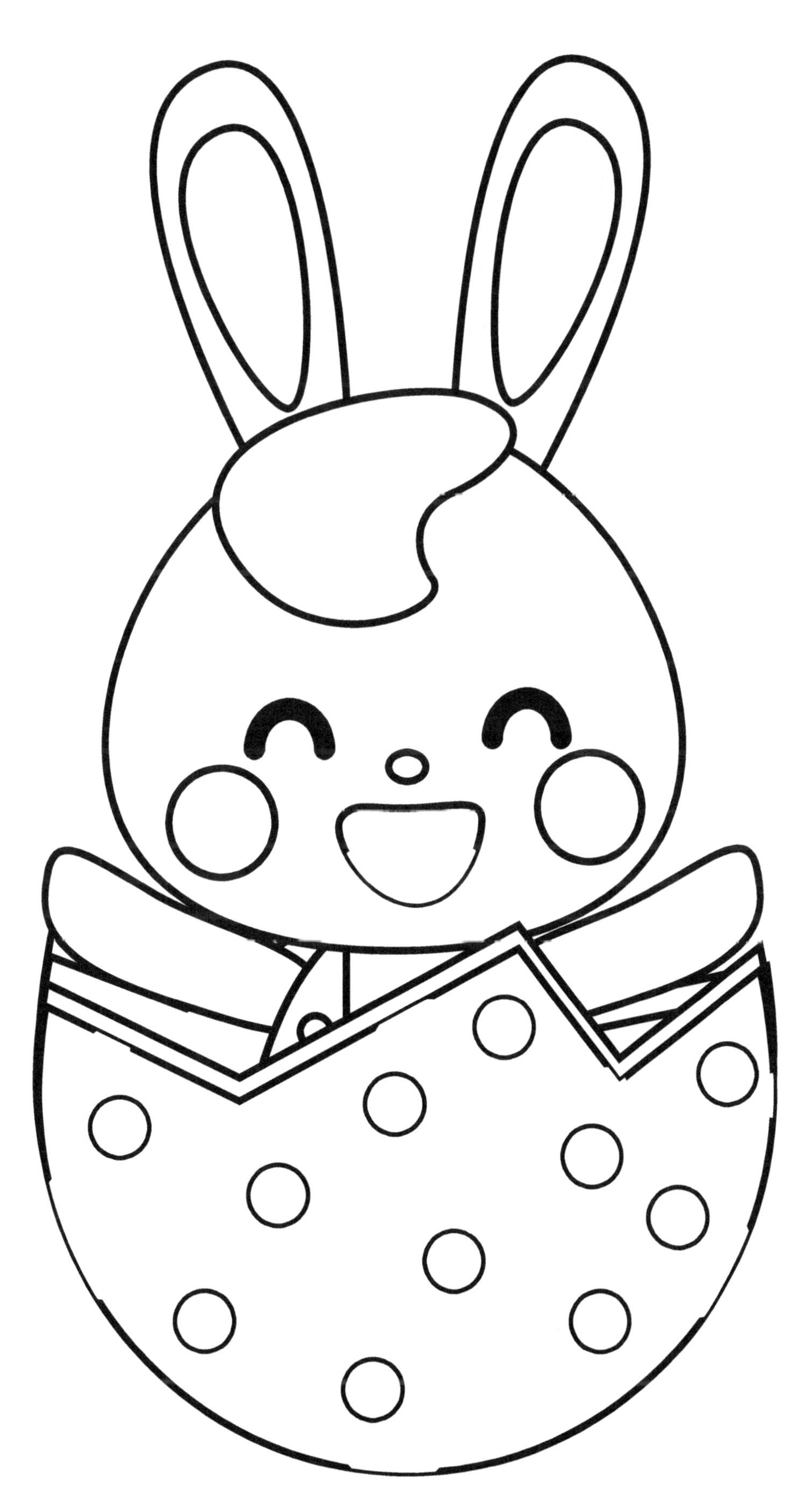

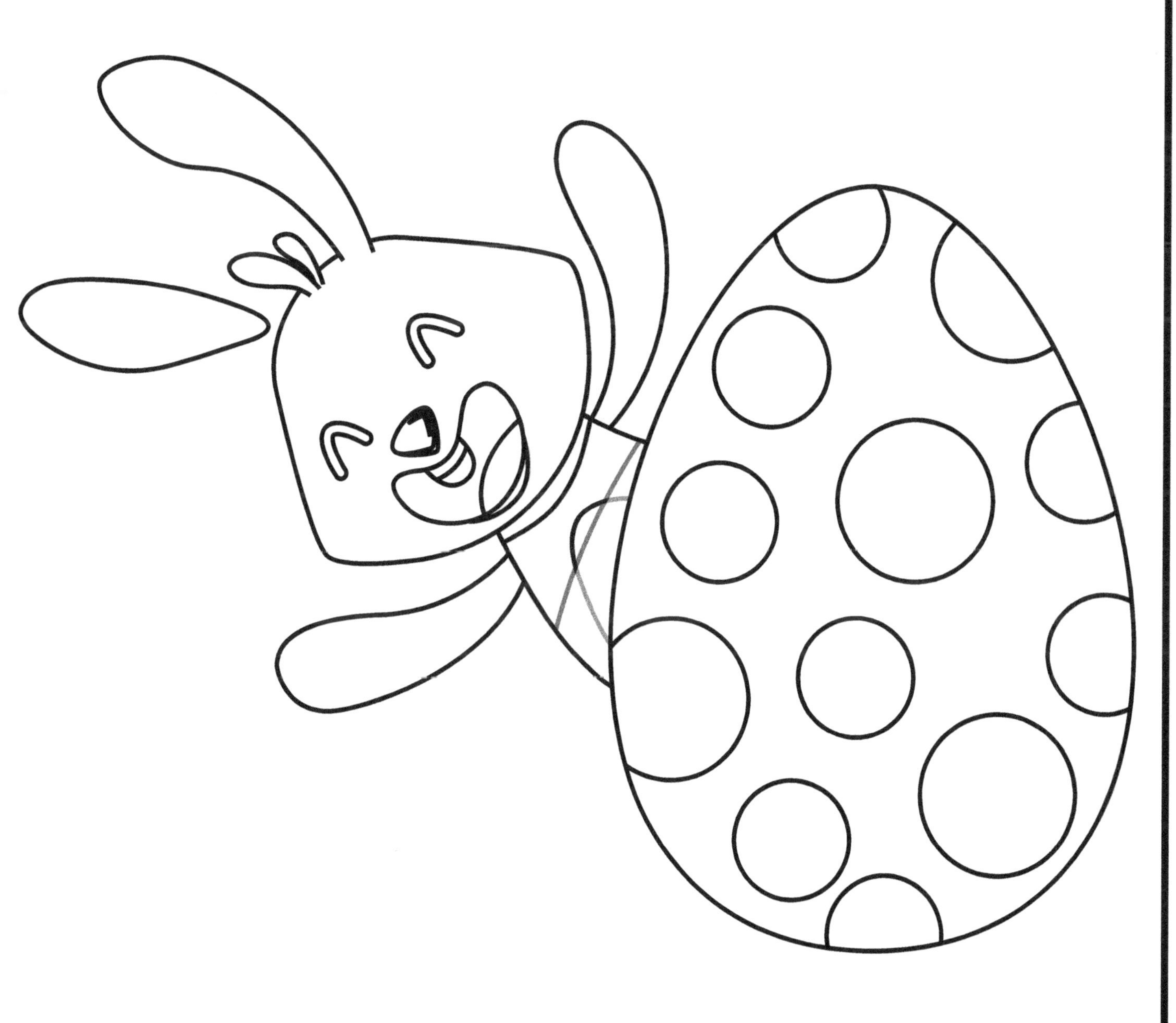

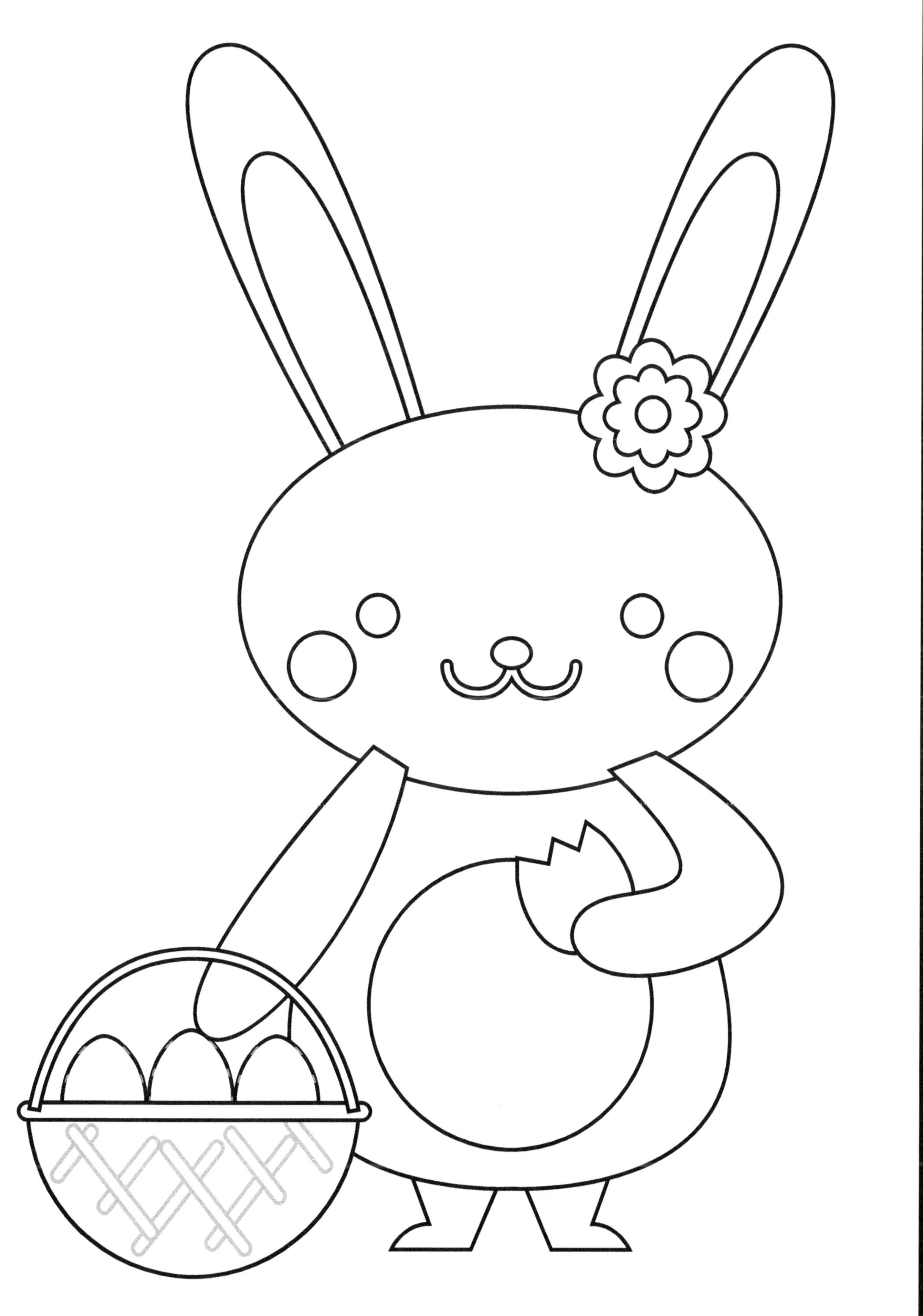

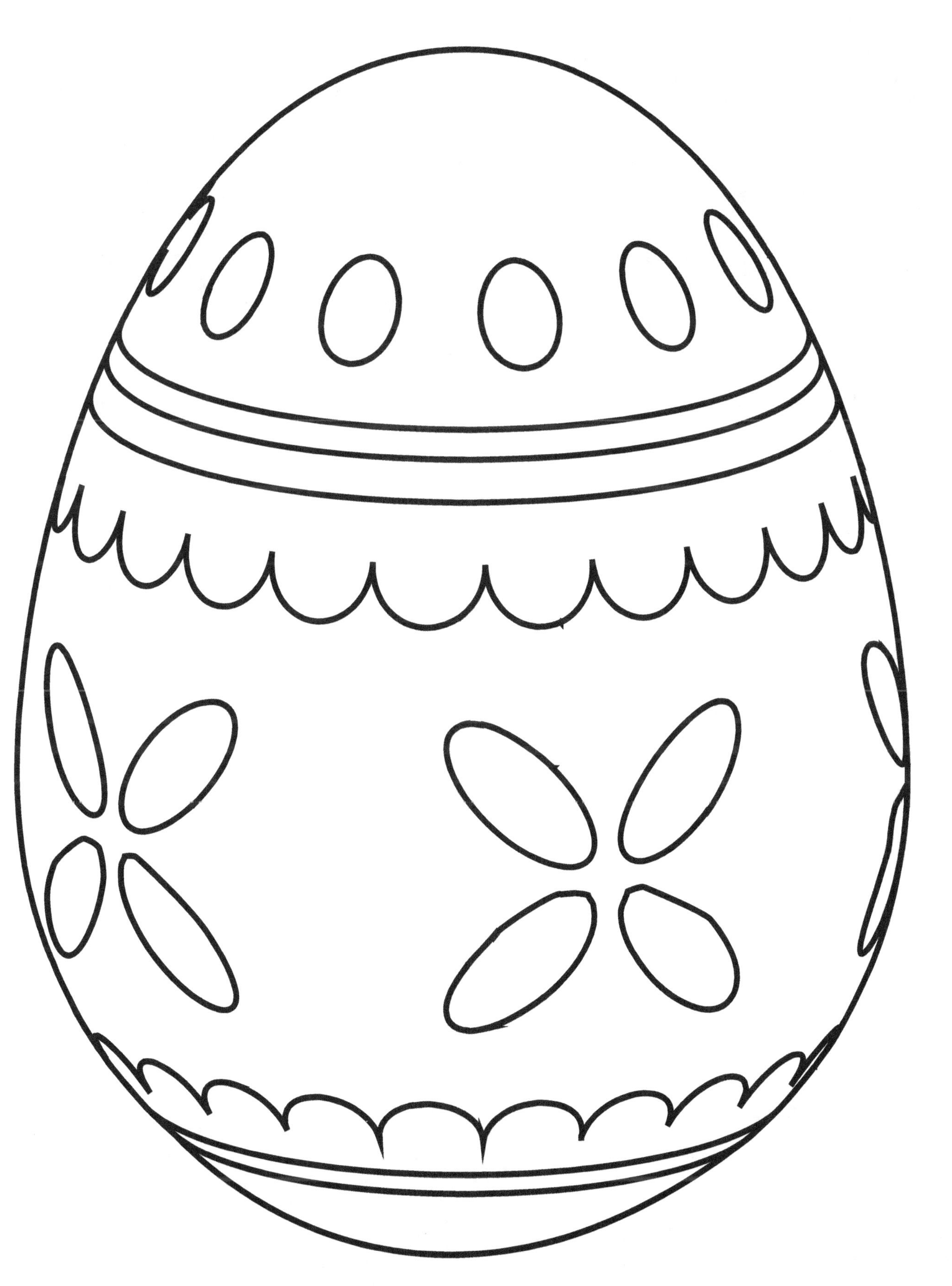

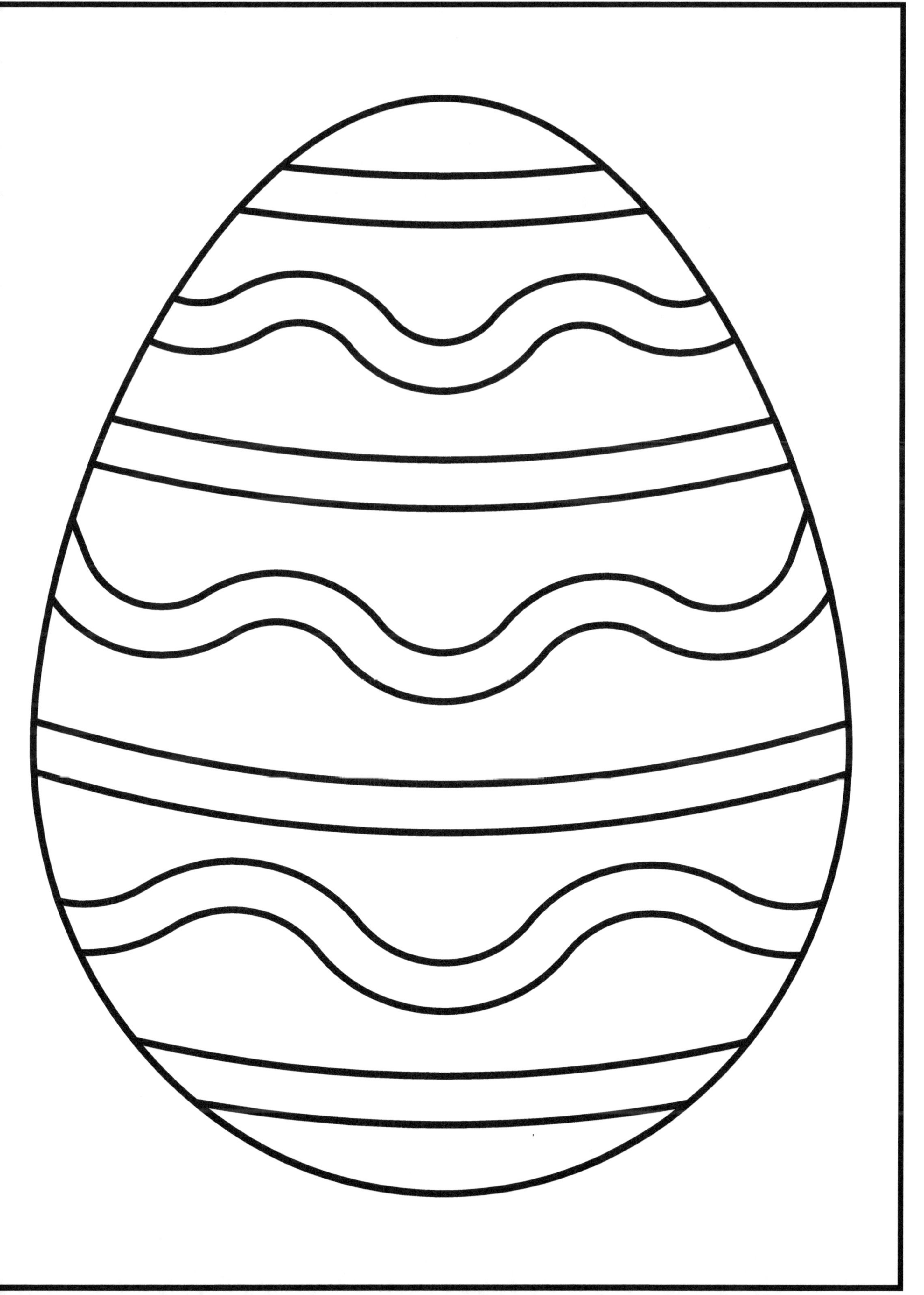

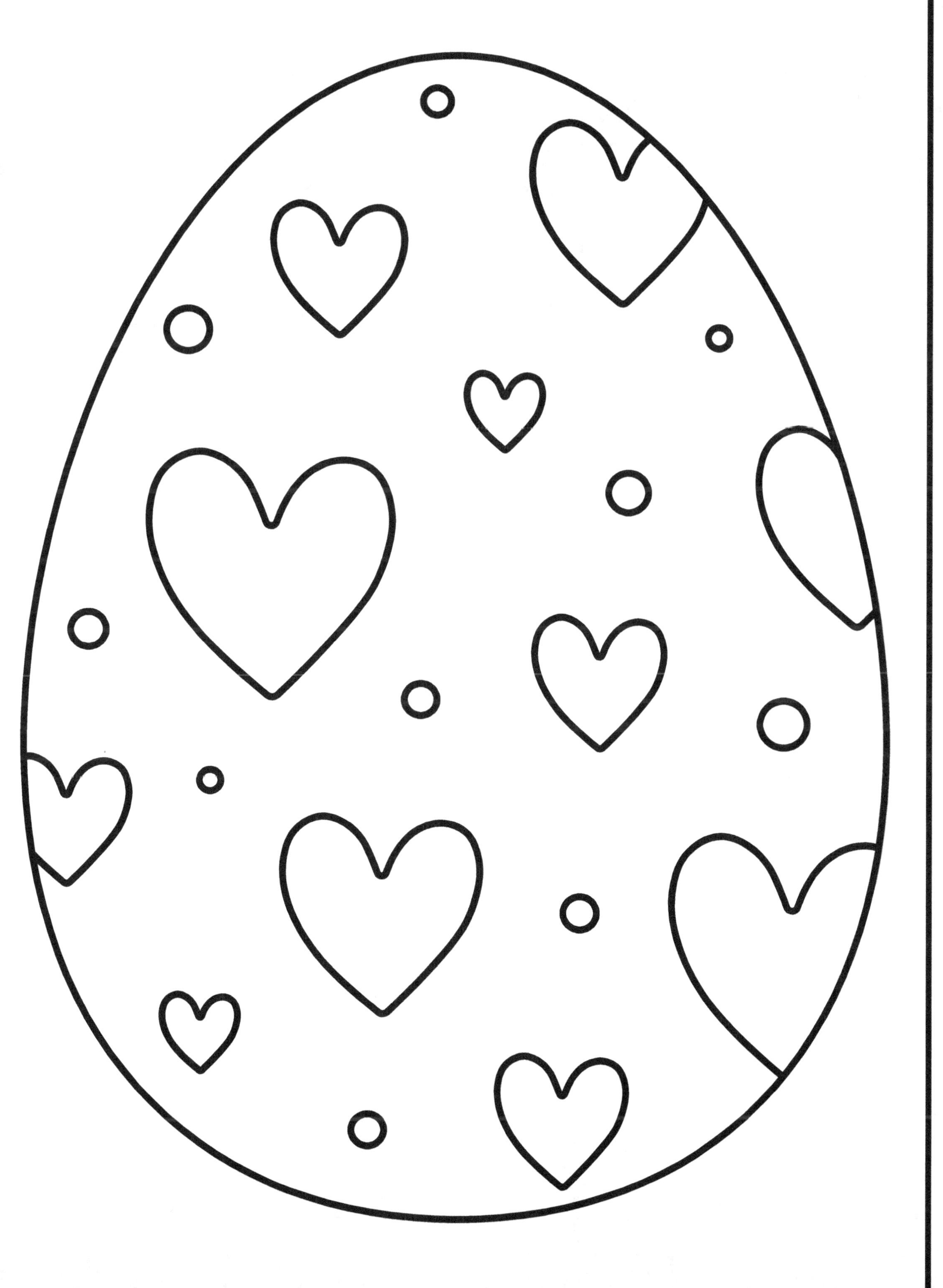

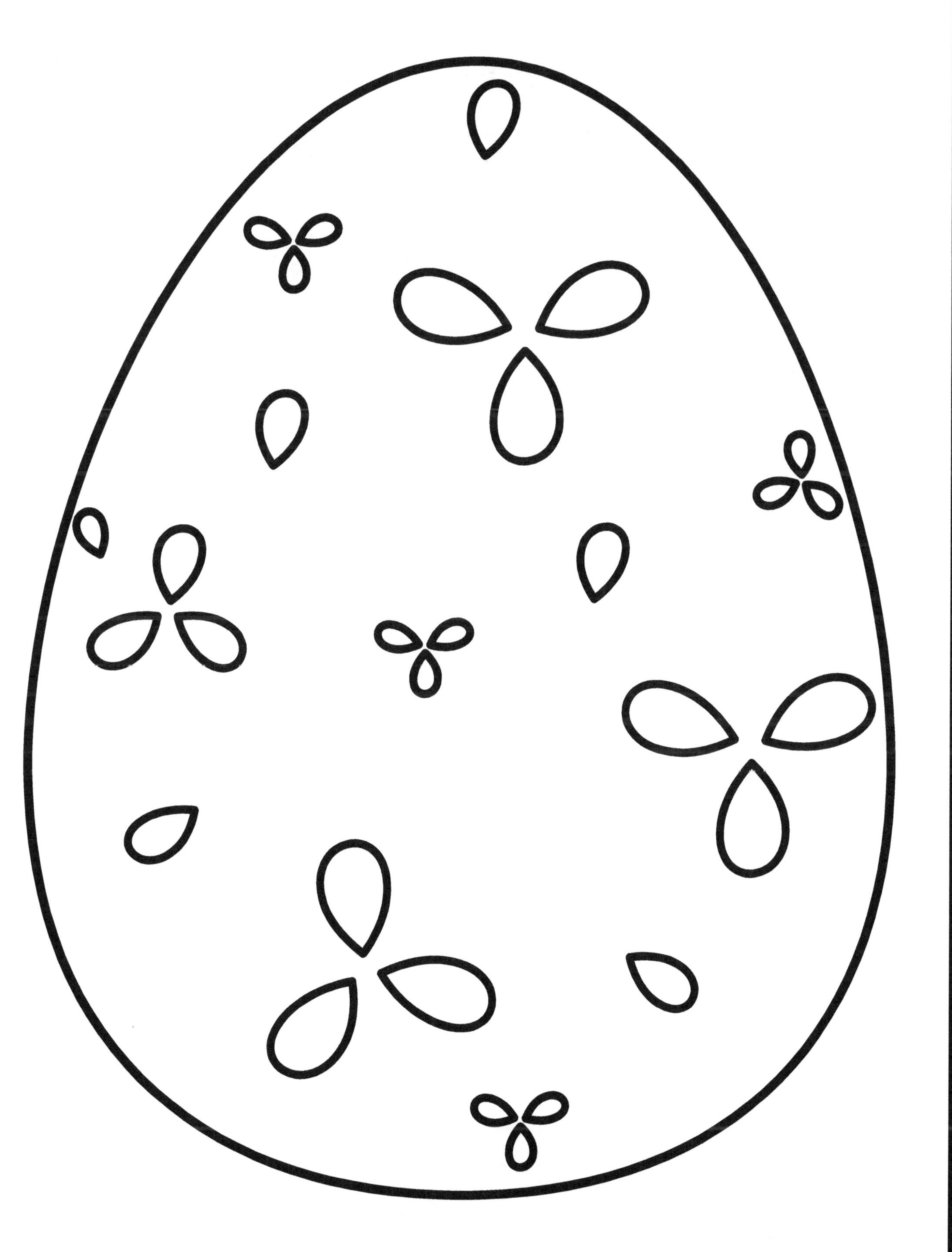

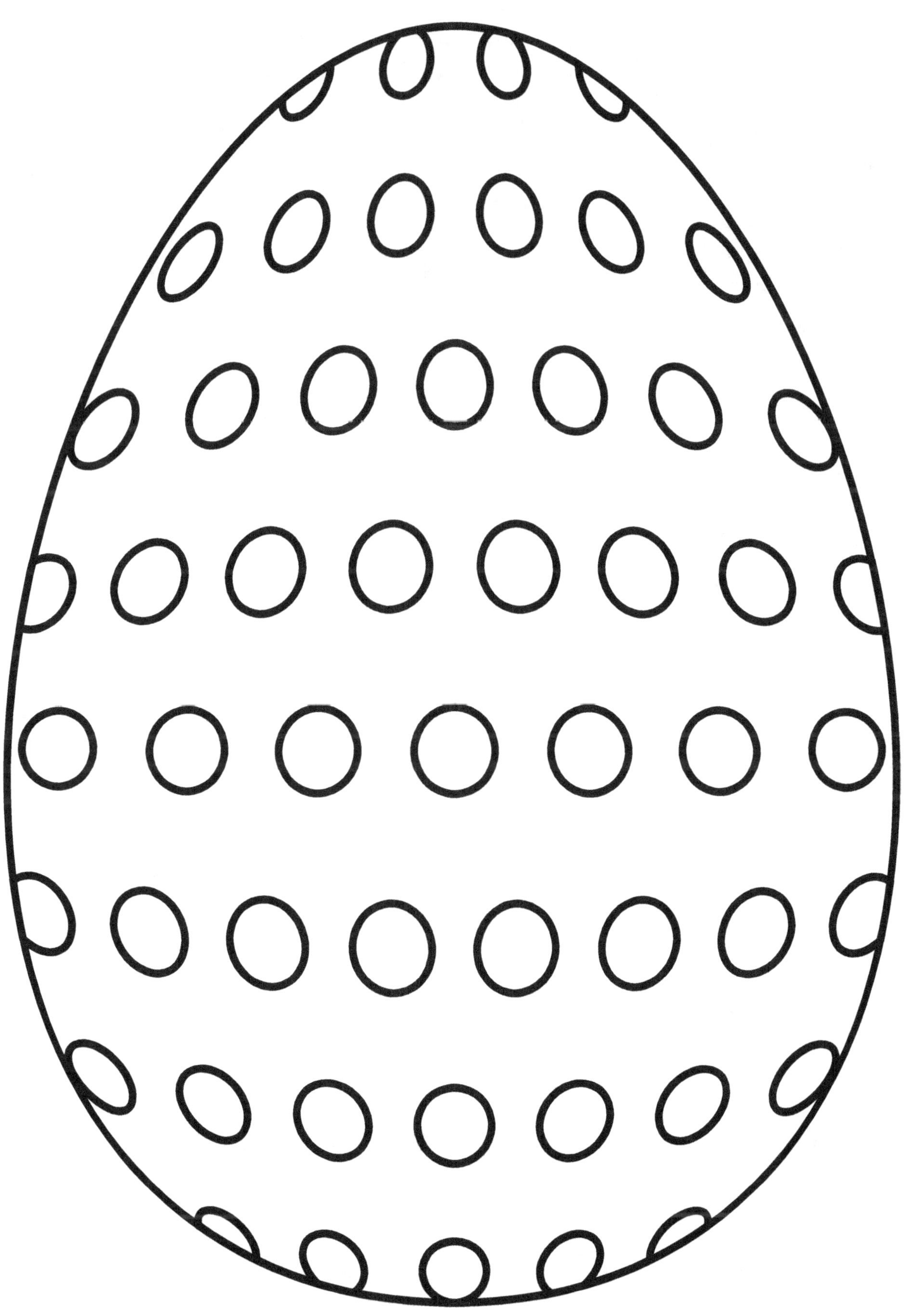

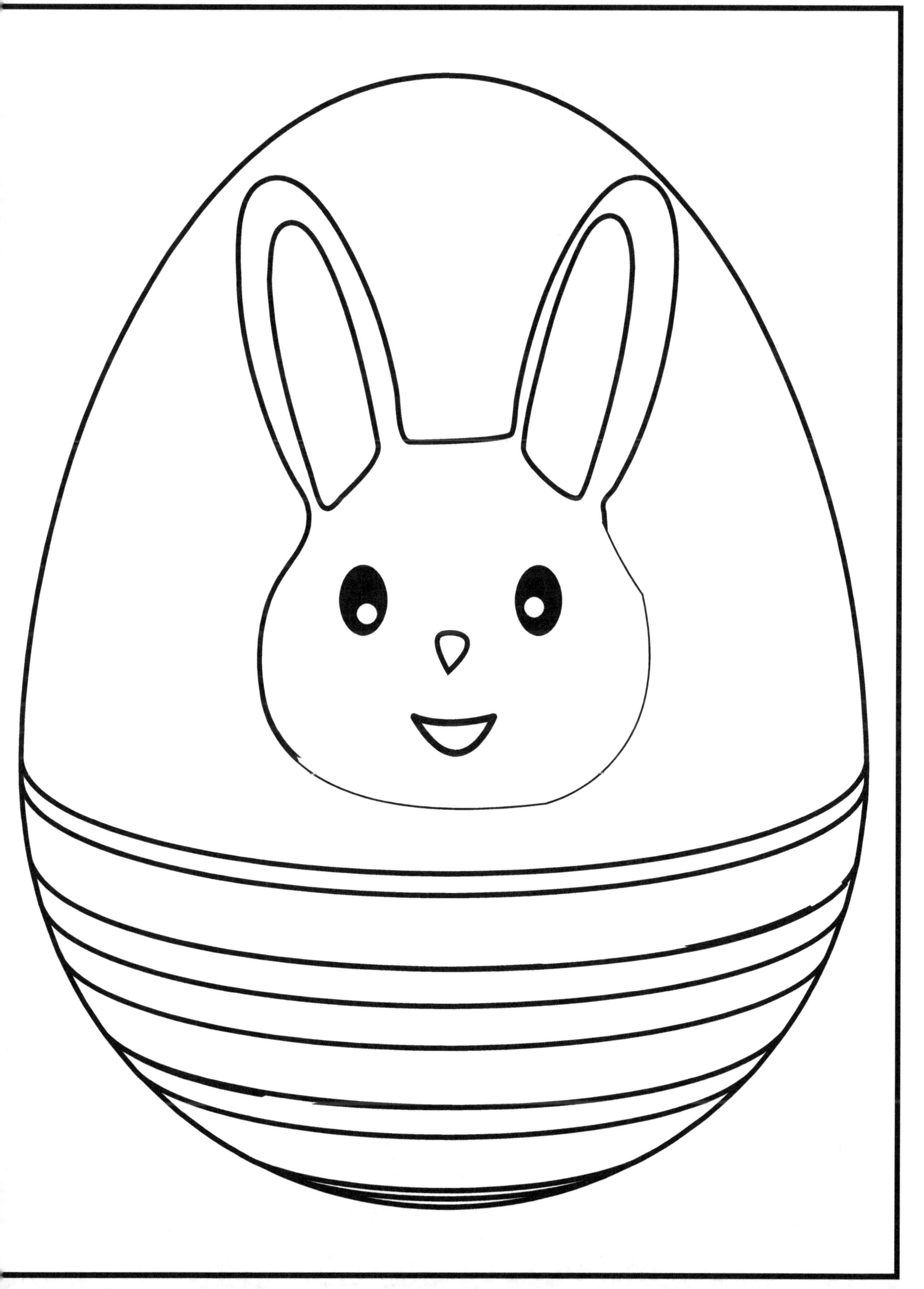

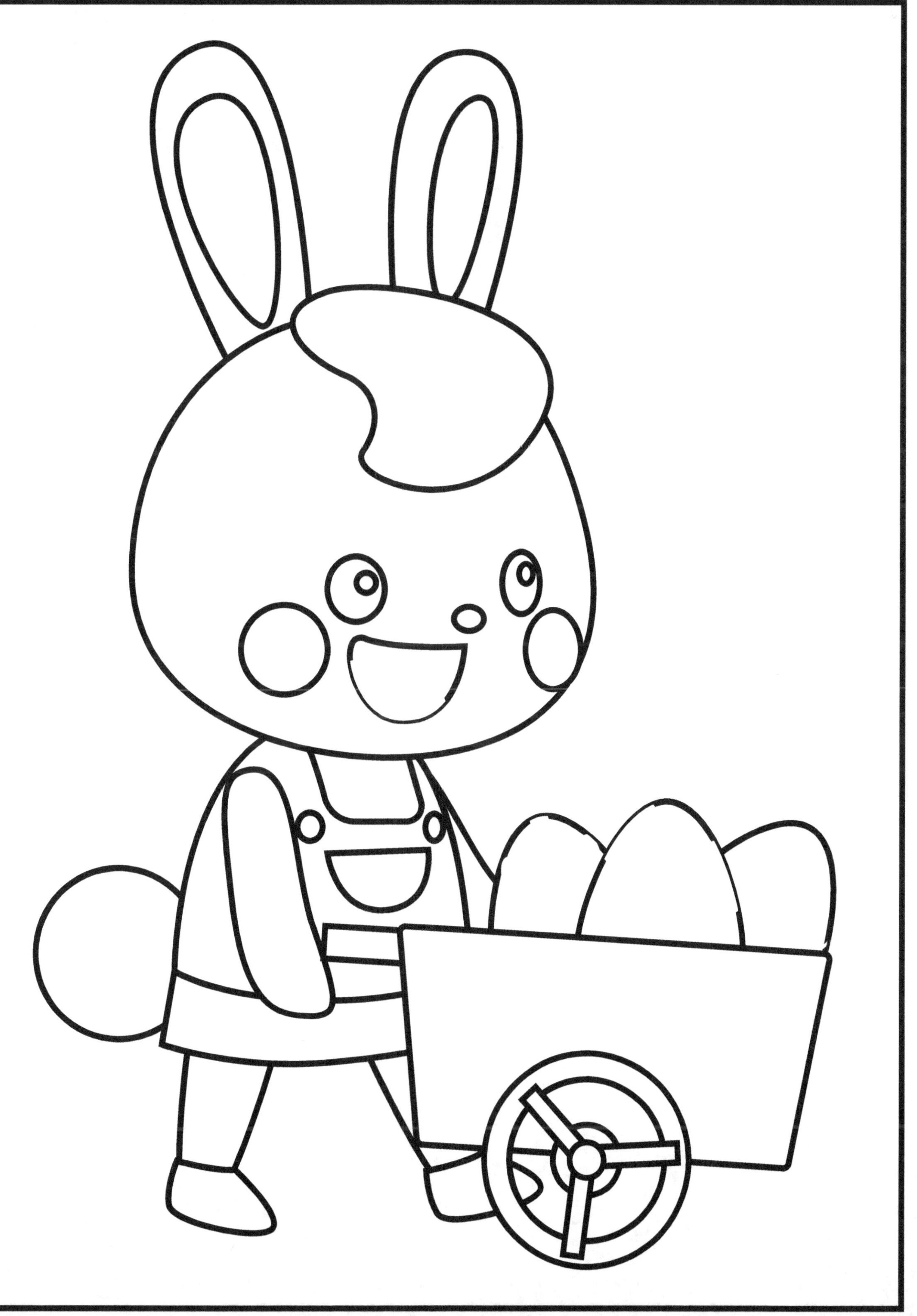

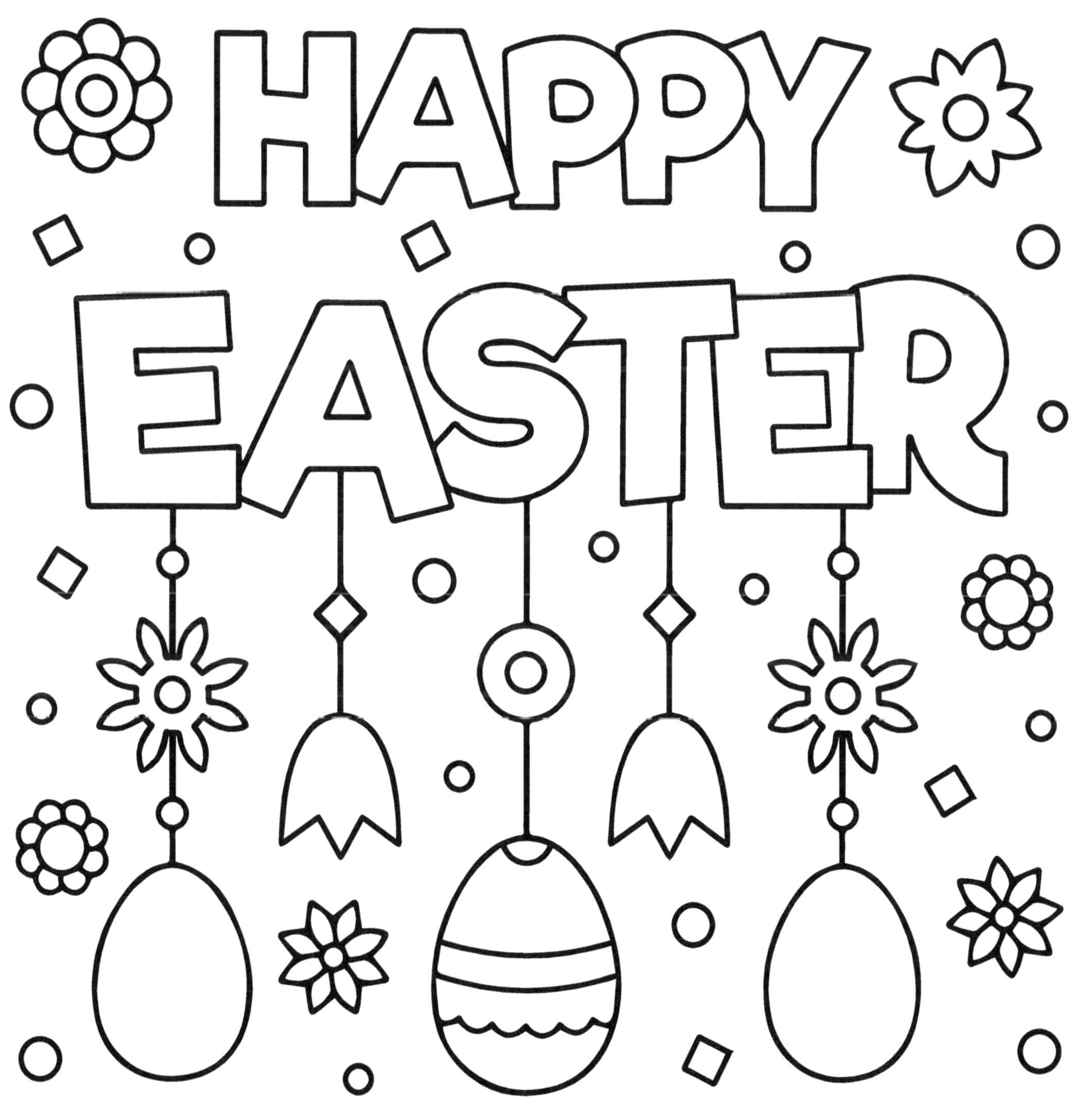

HAPPY
EASTER

Easter Egg

For emergency contact

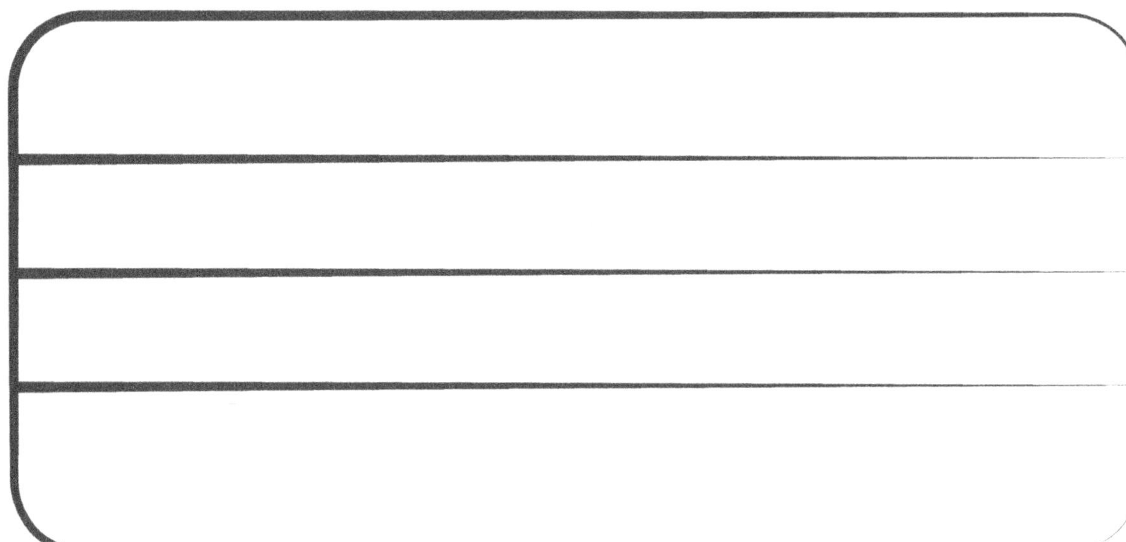

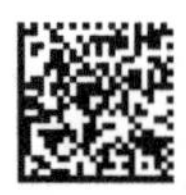